Homo Numericus

Homo Numericus

The Coming 'Civilization'

Daniel Cohen

Translated by Steven Rendall

polity

Originally published in French as *Homo numericus. La 'civilisation' qui vient*
© Editions Albin Michel – Paris 2022

This English edition © Polity Press, 2024

Polity Press
65 Bridge Street
Cambridge CB2 1UR, UK

Polity Press
111 River Street
Hoboken, NJ 07030, USA

ISBN-13: 978-1-5095-6021-9 – hardback

A catalogue record for this book is available from the British Library.

Typeset in 11 on 14pt Sabon
by Fakenham Prepress Solutions, Fakenham, Norfolk NR21 8NL
Printed and bound in Great Britain by CPI Group (UK) Ltd, Croydon

The publisher has used its best endeavours to ensure that the URLs for external websites referred to in this book are correct and active at the time of going to press. However, the publisher has no responsibility for the websites and can make no guarantee that a site will remain live or that the content is or will remain appropriate.

Every effort has been made to trace all copyright holders, but if any have been overlooked the publisher will be pleased to include any necessary credits in any subsequent reprint or edition.

For further information on Polity, visit our website:
politybooks.com

Thinking of Suzanne

Contents

Acknowledgements

This book has benefitted immensely from the friendly, in-depth re-readings by Roland Bénabou and Francis Wolff; constant encouragement by Gilles Haéri and Alexandre Wickham, an eternal friend; Alexandre Cadain's valuable insights and the care taken with my manuscript by Marie-Pierre Coste-Billon and her team at Albin Michel. I think of Roger Godino and Henri Weber, whose commentaries I would have so much liked to hear. This book is dedicated to Suzanne Srodogora.

Introduction

In one of the most striking episodes of *Black Mirror*, a hit British TV series, a young woman loses her husband in a car accident on the same day that she learns she is pregnant with his child. Thanks to artificial intelligence (AI), which combs through his telephone calls, videos, and emails, he is resuscitated digitally, perfectly, with his intonations, intuitions, replies to her questions, etc. The series' power is based on the fact that it seems to be only one step beyond what is currently possible. It explores our ability to accept the influence of new technologies, on the hypothesis that the latter's limits will be less technical than social and psychological.

The idea that the dead can be resuscitated by drawing on their 'history' is both totally terrifying and perfectly credible. The software programs powered by AI dive into the personality of their users, and, by recognizing the intonations of their voices, the complexion of their faces, and identifying the armature of their vocabulary, they grasp people's temperaments and aspirations. Much of the recruiting for a job or for admission to a university now takes place online. AI preselects, from a list of applicants that may run to many thousands of people, the few candidates who will have the good fortune to speak, in the last stage of the process, with a human evaluator. Even love does not escape being put through this mill. As the sociologist Eva Illouz brilliantly shows, applications such as Tinder make it possible to industrialize love relationships by reducing the amount of time spent on courtship, limiting love to 'just fucking'! Emotions, desires, and fears are subjected to new algorithms that wholly transform affective relationships. A new economy, a new sensibility, new ideologies: like the great transformation produced by the Industrial Revolution, the digital revolution is bringing about a radical revaluation of society and its representations.

In the new society that is dawning, the goal is no longer to buy objects such as vacuum cleaners or washing machines, but rather to consume one's own fantasies, whether individual or collective. In economic terms, we could say that the digital revolution is 'industrializing post-industrial society' – the latter term designating a world in which the essence of activity no longer consists in cultivating land or producing manufactured goods, but in taking care of human beings themselves, of their bodies and their fantasies. On the Internet, everything is done to ensure that people can be entertained, educated, cared for, or courted at the lowest possible cost.

In an utterly unanticipated way, the Covid pandemic has served as a catalyst for this great transformation. It is firms such as Amazon, Apple, and Netflix that have emerged victorious from this crisis – firms whose capitalization on the stock market exploded during the lockdowns. They made it possible to work from home and buy merchandise without having to go to a shop, to be entertained without going to a theatre or a concert hall. Digital capitalism's goal became clear to everyone: it is to reduce the cost of physical interactions to a minimum. To generate profit, it dematerializes human relationships.

Algorithms play, on the scale of society, the role that used to be played by the assembly line in the organization of industrial work. It is not only the management of bodies that is optimized; people's psyches are also 'Taylorized'. Search engines guide web users towards sites where they can find dating partners or opinions that are supposed to be well suited to them, thereby confining them in practice to new digital ghettos. Although obsessed by the search for an 'efficient' management of human relations, the new capitalism creates, in a completely contradictory manner, an irrational, impulsive *Homo numericus*. 'Too many images, sounds, and stimuli provoke concentration deficits, symptoms of hyperactivity, and addictive behaviours', Michel Desmurget writes in an appropriately titled book: *La Fabrique du crétin digital* ('The digital cretin factory'). Far from producing a new agora, a site for discussion where ideas are circulated and exchanged, social networks lead to a completely unforeseen radicalization of public debate. Hate-filled speech directed against adversaries has become the norm of these new 'conversations'. What is sought on the Net is not information, but beliefs that are consumed like an ordinary commodity, each individual finding in the great digital storehouse the truth that suits him, as in Pirandello's play.

Unless we lapse into a determinism maintaining that technology, and it alone, holds the key to civilizations, the current transformation cannot be understood if one fails to grasp the historical process of which it is an element. The digital revolution pushes to its peak the disintegration of the institutions that structured industrial society, as far as enterprises themselves, labour unions, political parties, or the media are concerned. This process is itself the direct result of the free-market shock of the 1980s, which sought to expand the marketplace and competition in every possible dimension, without mediations, without intermediary bodies. Working from home, which might prove to be Covid's most durable legacy, is part of a long process of externalizing tasks and individualizing remunerations. But in a subliminal way, digital society also draws on the counterculture of the 1960s and its critique of the verticality of power and institutions. Defeated by the free-market revolution, the spirit of the sixties wanders like a ghost through social networks, lending them a resolutely anti-system tone even if they have become the system. As the American sociologist Fredric Jameson said regarding modernity, the present transition offers a kind of 'compensation' for the political failure of the cultural revolution by adopting its language. The biblical Isaac could say: 'It's Dylan's voice and Thatcher's hand.'[1]

The digital human who inherits this strange filiation is caught in the trap of a society reduced to the aggregation of individuals trying to escape their isolation by constituting fictive communities. Nonetheless, the idea of a society offering every individual an opportunity to engage alone in countless parallel conversations is a myth that is exhausting to bear. The French *gilets jaunes* ('Yellow Vests') noisily made it clear that social solitude is the deepest ache there is (it is even the cause of suicides, according to Durkheim, the father of French sociology), and that virtual links do not heal us of the desire to live in flesh and blood among humans. 'People live beyond their psychic means', said the psychoanalyst Pierre Legendre. The observation is striking and can be generalized: in reality, people live beyond their means, period, whether those means are psychological or ecological. Reality, however, is never far away. One after the other, the Yellow Vests, the Covid pandemic, and then the war in Ukraine have reminded us, in their own way, that life is not a video game.

In its own perverse way, however, the digital revolution also sketches an exciting path: the one that leads to a world in which everyone deserves to be listened to. It explores a new way of living that is unprecedented in the history of civilizations – that of a society that seeks to be simultaneously horizontal and secular: without the verticality that still prevailed in industrial society and without the religiosity of agrarian societies; closer, perhaps, to the hunters and gatherers, but without the superstitions, if possible.

It's a long road, simply to understand what such a utopia means. We have to take up this challenge and make the unheard-of imaginative effort of conceiving a desirable society with the means given to us by the society we want to leave.

Part I

The Digital Illusion

1

Body and Mind

Terminator

Archimedes asked for a lever to lift the Earth. In its turn, the digital age, like the industrial revolutions that preceded it, aims at a simple objective: making human labour more 'productive'. However, the fundamental difference from the revolutions of the past consists in this: it is human beings themselves who are both the lever and the mass to be lifted. An exciting and terrifying dialogue between two eminent experts on intelligence, Yann Le Cun and Stanislas Dehaene – who seem influenced as much by science fiction as by biology – shows us what is going on:

> SD: Personally, I'm a believer in the interface between the brain and machines. I believe that connecting the brain to supplementary systems by means of rapid interfaces will allow it to be more effective. And this combination will be difficult to beat for a long time.
>
> YLC: Yes!
>
> SD: A chip that is grafted onto the brain injects signals sensitive to the direction of the magnetic field, and suddenly the rat orients himself better in space, as do pigeons.

YLC: I don't believe in replacement, but rather in displacement. Cosmic evolution always moves toward more complexity. Intelligence evolves but doesn't have to remain strictly human.

Reading this dialogue, people could be convinced that the film *Terminator* had an influence on scientific thought – except that the idea of allowing human brains to communicate with machines is no longer illusory. In 2018, an implant placed in the brain of a quadriplegic enabled him to control, by means of thought, an exoskeleton that helped him to walk.[1] Armies all over the world are not the last to take an interest in this promise of a mixture of human flesh and silicon ... The newspaper *Le Monde* reported an incredible account of an 'augmented soldier' with chips placed under his skin that allowed him to send or receive information at a distance in a theatre of war. By 2030, these developments might take the form of 'operations on ears to enable them to hear very high or very low frequencies, or of implants making it possible to take control of a weapons system'.[2]

Aware of the debates that this evolution might provoke, the French Comité d'éthique de la défense (Defence Ethics Committee), composed of eighteen civilian and military members, took the trouble to formulate about twenty recommendations. For each 'augmentation' of soldiers, a risk/benefit analysis will have to be conducted; it would involve taking into account the side effects that 'a certain number of rays or electronic components might have on the body'. The reversibility of these augmentations will also have to be studied. 'Any augmentation that is thought to be of such a nature as to [...] provoke a loss of humanity or would be contrary to the principle of the dignity of the human person' should be prohibited. The military's ethics committee also prohibits any 'cognitive augmentations [that] might affect the free will that the soldier must have in battle'.

Similarly, 'eugenic or genetic practices that would endanger the re-integration [of the soldier] into society upon his return to civilian life' should also be proscribed. This will certainly reassure us!

We must take seriously these moments in history when science fiction intersects with the military imagination. Battlefields have always provided theatres of experimentation for the most revolutionary technologies. The Internet and GPS are recent examples that have emerged from the files of the United States' Department of Defense. But technologies are not adopted and developed in a void; they have to satisfy a social need. Google Glasses were a technological marvel that flopped. Facebook, on the other hand, was a gadget for immature male students (making it possible to select the prettiest girls on the campus) that has conquered the world!

In both cases, we must ask ourselves why. Describing the way the emerging society turns our lives and mentalities upside down requires us to avoid two symmetrical traps. The first involves attributing to technologies an autonomous power they do not generally have. The second consists, inversely, in underestimating their disruptive capacities, the shortcuts that they lead us to take, often in response to imbalances they themselves provoke. The gap between the inventors' initial intentions and the use to which their inventions are ultimately put can be gigantic. Our uncertainty when faced by inventions as radical as AI, as in the past with the printing press or television, is the result of, among other essential things, a simple fact: societies are not inanimate beings. They respond to new technologies in ways that cannot be fully predicted.

To describe the digital revolution is not to tell the story of a destiny announced or undergone. It is to explore its virtualities, to gauge its risks, in order to acquire the means to dominate it. That is the true challenge.

Reason and Emotions

When humans began working on assembly line, they became machines. Today, with AI, it's the machine that is becoming human. It can increase our cognitive or mechanical abilities, but it can also lead to making us dispensable. There are no longer any ticket-punchers at the entrances to tube stations, and no doubt there will soon no longer be any cashiers at supermarket exits. Confronted with the formidable power of computers and AI, what advantage can humans claim to have? Will we have to implant electrodes in humans' heads to help them keep their position? Or will humans specialize in the tasks that the machine is not capable of performing: loving, laughing or weeping, at the risk of letting algorithms take charge of the system's collective intelligence? Answering these questions requires nothing less than a return to the questions that philosophy and biology have been exploring for centuries: what are humans, no longer relative to gods or animals, but relative to the technologies they have themselves produced?

A simple observation: a human is a body and a mind, while a machine is neither one nor the other. A human is a mind, first of all: he produces, spontaneously, theories about the world. By the age of 9 months, a baby has assimilated the laws of gravitation: he throws his toys to see if they fall as expected. Very early, a child differentiates between inanimate objects and living beings. After seeing two or three elephants, the child immediately grasps the concept of this strange animal and can recognize it in his picture books. A machine cannot do these things spontaneously. It needs to scan several million elephants to recognize just one. A driver completely inexperienced on a mountain road knows that he has to avoid the ravine, even if he has never before fallen into it. A machine needs millions of virtual crashes to understand that it has to keep the car on the road. It isn't as brilliant as one might imagine it to be!

The specificity of humans is to produce theories about everything: about wind, stars, themselves ... Life is too short for our comprehension of the world to be deduced only from lived experiences. We need concepts to orient ourselves in a world filled with mysteries. As we are reminded by Richard Thaler, an economist who received the Nobel Prize for his work on behavioural economics, humans have limited time and limited intelligence. They employ intuitive rules to judge and decide. We do not live in a world like Bill Murray's in the film *Groundhog Day* (1993). The character played by Murray wakes every morning to re-live the same day. Once he has understood the totality of the world's possibilities, he can act knowing the consequences of his acts and win the heart of his colleague, played by Andie MacDowell. The hero of Milan Kundera's book *The Unbearable Lightness of Being* (1984) asks himself a question of the same kind: 'Is it better to be with Tereza or to remain alone? A human can never know what he has to know because he has only one life, and he can't compare it to earlier lives or rectify it in later lives.' Kundera concludes that human life is like a drama in which you have to act without ever having rehearsed it. You can't go back in time to correct your errors. You have to act, relying on your intuitions alone.

The theory of the mind

Humans do not think alone, they think with others, in conversation with them. Francis Wolff speaks of the 'dialogic' nature of man.[3] It is in these discussions with other people, when demands are made on us by our interlocutor, that we feel awake. Reason becomes sharper when we seek to construct arguments to convince others, and that at the same time allow us to fight our own prejudices. Moreover, it is in the form of an imaginary dialogue with ourselves that we organize our thought, in solitude. The mirror stage, when the child recognizes himself in the mirror's reflection, is in this respect crucial: he sees himself as he understands he is seen by others. Humans share this trait with primates. A chimpanzee looking into a mirror removes the confetti that has been put on his forehead. In the ape, there is also a zone of the brain that lights up when he is shown a film in which his fellows appear. It is amusing to note a curiosity stressed by the biologist Alain Prochiantz: shown a Western by Sergio Leone, macaques react more than humans do![4] A strong activation of the prefrontal areas is observed in an ape when it is shown *The Good, the Bad, and the Ugly* – an activation that is completely absent *with humans*. But that probably tells us more about Sergio Leone's Westerns than it does about our simian cousins.

'I know that you think that I'm thinking about you', expresses a (partly contradictory) thought that only a human can conceive. The anthropologist Robin Dunbar has perfectly summed up what is at stake.[5] So-called first-order intentionality is defined as having the ability to reflect on the content of one's own mind, as is shown by the use of the verbs 'suppose', 'think', 'wonder', 'believe', etc. Most mammals and birds probably fit in that category. More interesting are the cases in which the individual is capable of representing the mental state of someone else, to say: 'I know that you like apricots.' This ability defines a higher level of intentionality, conventionally called 'second-order'. It is the equivalent of the stage that children reach around the age of 6, when they acquire for the first time what specialists in cognitive sciences call the 'theory of the mind'. They understand that other people can have ideas different from their own.

'I know that you think that I'm thinking about you' characterizes a third level of intentionality. How far can one go on like that? The economist George Loewenstein has given a very eloquent example of fourth-level intentionality: you broke your ankle and you would like your colleague to come and get you in a car [level 1]. You suppose that she knows that you are suffering [2]. But she herself is not sure that you know whether she knows it [3]. On the strength of this supposed ignorance, she doesn't come to help you. And that is what you reproach her for: pretending not to know your situation in order not to help you [4][6] (with the successive orders of intentionality indicated between square brackets).

Dunbar defends the idea that humans can aspire to a fifth-order intentionality. The fifth order corresponds to being able to say: I suppose [1] that you believe [2] that I want [3] you to think [4] that I intend to threaten you ... [5].

Shakespeare's genius makes us reach these summits. In *Othello*, Shakespeare uses four states of mind: Iago wants Othello to believe that Desdemona loves Cassio, and that Cassio loves her. But Shakespeare himself has to persuade the audience to believe all that. In addition – and this matters – he has to imagine everything himself; he must be capable of working – at a minimum – with a sixth-order intentionality: he wants the audience to understand that Iago wants Othello to believe ..., etc. Only a human (and not just any human!) is capable of such a feat.

In these mirror games with other people's thought, a quality emerges that is exclusively human: producing fiction. Animals simply can't understand what a story is – not only because they don't have the language for doing so, but because they wouldn't be capable of understanding what it is. If they had a language, they would take the story they are told at face value, being incapable of comprehending the account of a world that does not exist. With cognitive capacities limited to second-order intentionality, a chimpanzee could write and think 'Iago is going to leave', but it could not understand that in fact Iago would like it to be thought that he is going to leave. Only humans can produce a literature of the kind that we associate with culture. As Nancy Huston puts it magnificently in *The Tale-Tellers: A Short Study of Humankind*: 'No one has ever come across a human population that was content to live in reality – i.e. without religion, taboo, ritual, genealogy, fairy-tales, magic, stories – i.e., without recourse to the imagination, without confabulations.'[7] The first comparative advantage of humans, in the language of economists, is involved here: humans can invent a world that does not exist. The problem is that they can also believe that it does.

Because humans are both creative and credulous.

Descartes' 'Error'

To understand the potential role of machines in relation to humans, we must add another decisive element: a human is not simply a mind. Unlike machines, humans think in a body. As Miguel Benasayag perfectly sums it up: 'the body is the site of passions, drives, long-term memory; it is where the memory of my parents or grandparents is reincarnated'.[8] The idea that humans function like automatons, as people believed in the eighteenth century, or as an assemblage of units of information, as theorists of cybernetics suggest, is no longer current among researchers. 'It is the emotions that guide us toward food or a sex partner', says Benasayag. Beyond these carnal needs, the human species has a 'physical' desire to know. On the other hand, stress inhibits capacities for action. An individual who has suffered an intense emotional shock – for example, a bombardment – will be seized by panic on seeing a match burst into flame.[9]

In a book entitled *Descartes' Error: Emotion, Reason, and the Human Brain* (2006), Antonio Damasio shows that it is emotion that confers on living beings their capacity for action. To illustrate his remark, Damasio tells the story of a nineteenth-century medical case involving a certain Phineas Gage, whose archives have made it possible to reconstruct his destiny. Gage was the leader of a team building railways when, at the age of 25, his head was pierced by an iron bar in an accidental error while handling an explosive. The point of the bar, which passed through Gage's head, weighed 6 kilograms! Gage survived, and two months later he seemed to have recovered. He regained his senses of touch, hearing, and vision, but his temperament had changed. He became irreverent and swore (which he never did before), and he no longer showed respect for his friends. 'Gage's body was alive, but it was to be inhabited by a new soul.' Thus, it appeared to the medical profession that, following a cerebral lesion, one might lose respect for social conventions, even though neither the intellectual functions nor language had been altered.

Another surprising change in Gage's personality also occurred. He conceived a great many projects, but succeeded in realizing none of them. His ability to foresee the future had completely disappeared. One of Damasio's patients, Eliott, who had a brain tumour, experienced the same concomitance of troubles: despite intact mental abilities, he found it impossible to make decisions, to plan efficiently his activities in the coming hours. The lesion on the prefrontal cortex was again responsible for this. Eliott was able to know things, but could not feel them. He could elaborate sophisticated plans but was no longer capable of deciding which one to choose. Foreseeing an uncertain future and programming our actions according-ly, as well as regulating our life in society, thus seem to be deeply dependent on our ability to feel emotions, love or hate, stress or soothing calm. We humans have to 'feel' things before deciding what is good for us. Most important questions, like 'Must I accept this job, in this city?' are not settled with the help of a comparative list of advantages

and disadvantages. They are decided by the emotions that
they imprint on our body. It is the body that gives its
opinion, and says: 'Go for it!'

Spinoza was right

If, in a first book, Damasio points out 'Descartes' error', in
a second one he explains that 'Spinoza was right.' Baruch
Spinoza is the thinker who illuminates in the most striking
way this indivisible unity of body and mind. For him,
humans are not governed by reason but by desire, which he
designates as 'conatus': the effort to 'persevere in its being'.
Desire is not passion: the latter is born of an inappropriate
desire, connected with 'inadequate' ideas. If I am in love and
I'm dying of jealousy, it's because the relationship is wrong.
Wisdom consists in converting our passions into actions
that make us move forwards, that increase our ability to act,
by understanding what is good for us. Spinoza proposed a
typology of the affects on the basis of a simple dichotomy:
joy and sadness. Joy breaks out when someone increases
his abilities to act. Conversely, sadness occurs when he feels
deprived of the latter. People are usually not aware of the
causes that lead them to desire this or that. Nonetheless,
they are perfectly capable of associating their desires with
either external or internal causes. Thus, Spinoza defines love
as a joy that accompanies the idea of an external cause.[10]
The close link between the body and the mind is forged
in this association between an emotion and the idea that
accompanies it, gives it its meaning, and defines us as human
beings.

For biologists such as Damasio, emotions are regulative
mechanisms. Sadness reminds us of the value of life,
while fear alerts us to danger. According to Paul Ekman
(whose theories inspired the marvellous Disney-Pixar film
Vice-Versa), people generally recognize six primary emotions:

joy, sadness, fear, anger, surprise, and disgust. Ekman shows that these emotions are found in all cultures. He himself studied the tribes of Papua – New Guinea. When he showed his interlocutors photos of faces expressing each of the six basic emotions, all of them were immediately recognized. He inferred from this that the primary emotions are predetermined, which is also confirmed by the fact that people who are congenitally blind, and thus have no visual experience, smile and weep exactly like sighted people.

Immersion in society later fabricates moral emotions. Similarly, guilt, shame, and gratitude play a regulative role in life in society. Guilt arises when we worry about the consequences of our own acts on others.[11] Shame marks the weight of social judgement – it expresses the fear of a divorce between one's personal values and those of others. Finally, gratitude testifies to a sense of obligation to others, which promotes empathy, compassion, and generosity. Moral emotions are the regulators of life in society.[12]

The limits of human reasoning

Inclined as we are to feel these bundles of emotions, our reasoning is not as analytical as we would like to believe it is. Our stubborn propensity to produce theories, to make the world that surrounds us the subject of a narrative, ends up betraying us. Thus, the psychologist Daniel Kahneman, who received the Nobel Prize for his works on behavioural economics, contrasts 'causal thinking' – haunted by the search for causes of the events that occur – with statistical thinking, which analyses the facts 'as they are'.[13] Causal thinking is reassuring, it is guaranteed always to succeed, Kahneman explains. Your neighbour gives you the impression that he is preoccupied and it won't take you long to imagine the cause: his wife has left him, he has lost his job, etc. If you talk about it with your concierge, your intuition will quickly be confirmed, no matter what it is. We don't reason in a 'neutral' manner, seeking an absolute truth. We start from conclusions in which we already believe, in order to find the path that validates them.

Causal thinking is consoling, because it makes the world intelligible, but it lays a trap for us, the trap of a falsely coherent thought. Trivial affirmations such as 'He failed because he lacked experience' or 'They succeeded because they had a charismatic leader' seem to us far more interesting than a cool statistical observation that concludes: 'Considering factors X and Y, they had one chance in three of passing the exam.' Causal reasoning makes us think that the world is much more predictable than it really is. We ridicule experts when they make mistakes, but we do so without recognizing that their task is often much more complex, more uncertain, than we are prepared to admit.

This attitude reflects our appetite for 'rapid' thought and our loathing for analytical, laborious thought, which requires us to compile figures, produce tests, and take care to avoid drawing hasty conclusions. In a book in which he assesses his own work, Kahneman gives names to these two systems of thought: system 1 moves quickly; system 2 takes the trouble to ponder the arguments, to verify the proofs.[14] Most of the time, we rely on system 1, which makes us seek desirable interpretations rather than those that would flow from the facts. The human mind, to which we owe modern science, biology, and quantum mechanics, is inclined above all to simplistic reasoning. We always need to be for or against something, and we prefer to jump to conclusions and stick to them. To be sure, we don't refuse to seek proofs of our ideas, but this quest is selective. It proceeds by eliminating the proofs that get in our way. System 1 is based on shortcuts that make it possible to reduce a complicated problem to a simple problem, at the risk of making errors in reasoning.[15] Thus, asked what, in a given group, the probability is that a warm person is a woman and a rigorous mind is a man, most people respond in accord with their stereotypes, without even taking the trouble to find out how many women and men the group contains (which would at least have the merit of making their prejudices depend on a probability calculus). It is up to system 2 to make the calculation, but it is slow and lazy, almost always asleep.

Artificial Intelligence

Machines have neither bodies nor feelings. They don't have minds, either: they don't have humans' creative imagination. As Marc Mézard explains perfectly, machines are not capable of extrapolating their knowledge to unknown situations.[16] However, they do have a few advantages. They can carry out operations that are totally inaccessible to ordinary mortals, like searching, in a fraction of a second, millions of pages to find a quotation. In the case of games of chess or Go, an AI machine can learn in a few hours how to explore acres of possibilities that exceed the abilities of the world's best players. The machine can play an incalculable number of games, infinitely more than any human could ever play. Yann Le Cun, commenting on the defeat of one of the greatest Go players, makes this illuminating remark: 'Humans don't play Go well' – meaning that the game is actually too sophisticated to allow humans to deviate from the main lines established by tradition. In contrast, AI can play a virtually infinite number of games to 'discover' winning strategies, like Bill Murray in *Groundhog Day*. AI is an intelligence of memorization: it functions by learning the possible situations, without concepts to theorize them.

Serge Abiteboul has summarized 'algorithmic thinking' on the basis of an eloquent example, that of ants. Looking for food, ants use a rather simple algorithm to get their bearings

in space. Scouts go off at random in several different directions. When one of them finds food, it returns home, leaving
a trail behind it, like Tom Thumb: it secretes 'pheromones'
that attract other ants. The ants that follow the first one
leave behind them pheromones that 'reinforce' the attractiveness of the path. If a path is shorter, those who take it will
make more round-trips, further reinforcing its attractiveness.
Without any awareness of itself or of the group, even in the
very distant sense that humans may give this term, ants offer
a solution to the only question they pose: where to go to find
food. In the same way, algorithms note that one path is more
promising than another without understanding anything
about what it means. Algorithms associate preferences for
Proust and for Dostoyevsky without any knowledge of literature; they limit themselves to noting that those who love
one also love the other. That is an idiotic intelligence that is
at work in reality.

Learning to learn

AI enables a machine made of metal and electrical wires to
recognize an image; to transcribe a voice from one language
to another; to make a car drive itself, automatically; to play
chess, Go, video games ... Thanks to the exponential growth
of computers' power of calculation, spectacular progress
has been made by constructing algorithms that mimic the
structure of the human brain.[17] The latter contains 86 billion
neurons, as many as the number of stars in our galaxy. But
it is not so much their number that matters as the quality
of the connections established between them.[18] Each neuron
is connected to a thousand others through junctions called
synapses, used with variable frequency and intensity. Unused
connections are eliminated, and, conversely, when two
neurons are stimulated at the same time, the synapses create
or reinforce the links connecting them. They form the basis

for our memory and our personality, retaining the trace of the moments that have punctuated our lives.[19]

Where does modern AI come from? The first experts initially stressed an 'arborescent' logic. The latter seeks to define the tree of all the possible combinations: if I play A, then I will be able to play B or C. Thus, before playing A, we must first understand what B and C mean, which leads us to reflect also on the meaning of D, E, F, and G, which will make B and C possible ... Specialists speak of this research project as 'good old-fashioned AI' (GOFAI). It is thanks to this ability to reason that the Deep Blue machine defeated the chess champion Garry Kasparov, evaluating the possibility of about 200 million positions on the chessboard per second, and using a relatively classic technique of arborescent research.

This method has, however, been revealed to be far too fastidious, even for computers. Rather than seeking to reproduce all the possible sequences of a move made on a chessboard, specialists in AI have shifted gears, trying to imitate the manner in which the human brain educates itself. This is the method called 'deep learning', which takes its inspiration from neuronal networks in order to understand humans' learning processes. Each time a computer discovers a strategy that makes it advance (by leading it to win a game), it remembers winning combinations, as synapses do in human beings, and it can construct its own learning curve. The machine is taught to recognize a cat by showing it millions of them and by giving it a 'reward' when it succeeds. The same goes for chess games. So-called 'unsupervised' learning goes still further. It lets the machine solve problems by itself (without a pre-existing library of games won), giving only the result 'yes' or 'no' depending on whether it wins. This is the method at the origin of the successes of AlphaGo Zero, which has defeated the best Go players in the world. Very recently, it has also been learned that an AI conceived by a start-up in Paris, NukkAI, defeated the eight best bridge players in the world. This complex card game was 'one of the last ramparts of resistance to AI'.[20]

Yann Le Cun, one of the pioneers in this domain, also developed similar neuronal networks in order to create an automatic system to recognize signatures on cheques. In 2012, the Canadian physician Geoffrey Hinton used 'deep learning' to win an international contest to recognize images of cats. He was quickly poached by Google to work on its Google Brain project. That was the beginning of the flow of researchers towards this method. In 2014, Facebook's DeepFace project succeeded in recognizing an individual in two different photos – with a success rate of 97.35 per cent, the same as a human! Facebook, which has the largest photo gallery in the world at its disposal, can henceforth offer to find friends of whom you may have lost sight, apparently with a high rate of success. Errors in voice recognition have also become very few, below the threshold of 5 per cent!

Machines driven by AI are thus extraordinarily powerful when the rules of the game are clear: recognizing a cat or a squirrel because millions of photos already identified enable it to be trained; and playing chess because at the end the game is won if the enemy king is checkmated. However, for Yann Le Cun, 'no matter how powerful they might be, such machines have neither common sense nor a conscience' – at least 'not yet', he adds. Common sense is called upon to arbitrate in ambiguous situations, when there is neither a good nor a bad answer written in a book. A machine could kill a human in order to get a cup of coffee for that same human, if he appeared to be an obstacle to carrying out its mission. Like Phineas Gage after the iron bar passed through his brain, the machine does not grasp the subtleties of the social game: how does one say 'no' to someone without hurting him? Does one hold a crystal glass in the same way that one holds an iron bar? Can one safely jump from the fifth floor of a building? All the machine lacks is what we humans call emotions.

'I would consider my career a success', Le Cun concluded, 'if we were to succeed in constructing machines as sharp as a rat or a squirrel.' AIs are less intelligent than a cat, whose brain has 760 million neurons and 10,000 billion synapses and, a fortiori, less intelligent than a dog, with its 2.2 billion neurons. For Le Cun, the only question is how long it will take to build machines that approach the energy frugality of the human brain. This frugality has to do with the fact that only a small number of neurons are active at the same time. It is the avenue to be explored for the systems of the future. On the scale of its owner, the brain nonetheless remains a huge consumer of energy. If, like the great apes, humans had not invented cooking, and had continued to eat a diet based on leaves and wild berries, they would have to spend 9 hours a day feeding themselves to provide the calorie intake necessary for the physiology of their brains. Without the Promethean capture of fire, the human adventure would be entirely different.

Wisdom

Thus, it seems possible to outline what an 'efficient' distribution of tasks between humans and machines might look like. The tasks that require 'common sense', notably in relations with other humans, would be assigned to humans, and those that require statistical, laborious work would be assigned to machines. The sensitivity of the relation to the other, whether amorous or commercial, would be assigned to humans, and the calculation of the conditions that make it probable that an encounter will succeed would be assigned to machines. Finally, creativity in the sciences or the arts would be assigned to humans, while routine tasks that implement protocols for managing ordinary situations would be assigned to machines.[21]

All this seems fine: why be bored stiff answering the same question over and over if a robot can do it? Why deprive oneself of the databases that enable us to evaluate the chances that a romantic or professional liaison will succeed? This is the problem. Humans are malleable, they adapt to their environment. What constitutes their strength in the natural world becomes an immense weakness in a system constructed to manipulate them. If algorithms take charge of statistical thought, Kahneman's system 2, the risk is that they will leave humans prisoners of system 1 alone, that of imagination and prejudices, which moves them farther away from 'wisdom'. As Spinoza would put it, wisdom is a 'third kind of knowledge', or, as Kahneman would say, a system 3. In this system, we know instinctively what is true, without reflecting – that the square root of 4 is 2, thus transcending systems 1 and 2. That is not the path on which we are led by social networks, which are far more likely to halt us at level 1 of our affects, imprisoning us in our prejudices.

2

Stultify and Punish

Wild Thought

In any case, the digital revolution is proceeding. It is taking its place in a long line of radical innovations that have turned human ways of thinking upside down. First, the invention of writing set an ineradicable seal on the break between 'wild thought', as Lévi-Strauss calls it, and societies in which History, as a cumulative process, is established by means of writing. On the cusp of the modern world, printing also provoked a veritable intellectual revolution, promoting freedom of thought and contributing to the rapid expansion of the Reformation.

It was thought that AI would take its place in this glorious lineage, that it would help us think better both individually and collectively, and that it would multiply collaborative experiments such as Wikipedia. Alas, it seems safe to say that this promise will not be kept. The current transformation is leading to the birth of an individual marked by credulity and an absence of critical thinking. We expected Gutenberg, but it's television 2.0 that is being established.

In a classic of contemporary sociology, *Bowling Alone* (1995), the American sociologist Robert Putnam showed that the immense surge of individualism that seized Western societies after World War II owed a great deal to television. The considerable amount of time spent watching a television screen (4 hours and 50 minutes a day on average!) has led us to neglect friends, family, and associative life – what is called an individual's 'social capital'. Television has swept across all communities, from bowling clubs to PTAs, that used to provide the cement holding American social life together.

The magnificent work of Michel Desmurget, *La Fabrique du crétin digital* ('The digital cretin factory'), analyses from this point of view the malfunctions produced by the current revolution. The figures provided make one's head spin. From the age of 2, children spend almost 3 hours a day in front of their screens. Between 8 and 12, the time spent in front of tablets and laptops rises to 4 hours and 45 minutes a day, on average. From 13 to 18, it's 6 hours and 45 minutes a day. Thus, we reach a situation in which adolescents spend 40 per cent of their waking life in front of a screen! The psychic and affective life of these young people is punctuated by waves of sullenness and euphoria, shaped by addictive practices like online sexuality and manifested in deleterious effects on their nourishment and frequent risks of obesity. As analysed by Bruno Patino in *La Civilisation du poisson rouge*[1] or by Gérald Bronner in *Apocalypse cognitive*,[2] the capacity for attention among adolescents is severely damaged by channel hopping, impulsiveness, and impatience. Reading a book, which presupposes that the author is given time to introduce his characters or pursue a line of argument, is constantly interrupted by obsessive checking of one's mobile phone, which makes it almost impossible to remain focused on anything at all.

Marshall McLuhan, the high priest of this domain, said: 'The medium is the message.' The media are their own content, we look at television and not any particular film. In the same way, we don't know what we're looking at on our mobiles: 'scrolling', the indefinite unfolding of screens, sweeps us along in a totally addictive way. We are caught up by the scrolling itself, whether it's a sequence in which a child cries while watching *The Lion King*, or an adult watching news about the war in Ukraine.

The compulsive consultation of our mobile phones is labelled with a term that is now ubiquitous: FOMO ('fear of missing out'), which expresses the excruciating worry that we might miss something, whether it's a news item, gossip, or an opportunity. Without waiting for the impending synthesis of silicon and biology, the iPhone is already fabricating a genuine fusion of the human and the machine. The tactile interface creates a relational connection between the two, like the hard drugs that take possession of the brain and subject it to the need for their consumption. A German study cited by Gérald Bronner has shown that a telephone's ring lit up exactly the same area of the brain as did saying a person's first name![3] Even when the telephone is turned off but remains within view, the need to turn it on, to feel it in one's hands, is irresistible, like the injection that the heroin addict's brain commands him to give himself.

Adolescents' ability to attend to the real world has reached a historic low. According to a study cited by Patino, attention spans diminished by one-third between 2008 and 2015, from 12 seconds to 8 seconds! Desmurget also mentions Canadians (who are nonetheless ranked very high in traditional ratings of well-being and open-mindedness) as being among the primary victims of this development. Their wide-open spaces and rigorous winters have made them voracious consumers of digital culture, and this seems to have greatly reduced their attention span. The way of reasoning also changes in nature. 'Test and learn' has replaced logical explanation, as has AI itself: in the United States, students are no longer required to use cursive writing, but they must be able to use a keyboard. However, cursive writing plays a key role in the development of the brain and of motor skills. Of course, human beings have not always written, but the disappearance of written thought could have entirely unpredictable consequences for their way of reflecting.

Sean Parker, who was president of Facebook, was not afraid to admit that the firm sought nothing less than to 'exploit the vulnerability of human psychology'. What is at stake for all these social networks, from Facebook to TikTok, is winning this great 'battle for attention', no matter what the psychic consequences might be for the populations targeted. In a document entitled 'Facebook Files', a former employee of Facebook, Frances Haugen, has revealed that the company founded by Mark Zuckerberg was fully aware of the psychic troubles that it was producing. This whistle-blower, who is a graduate of Harvard and who had spent two years working for Facebook, gave the *Wall Street Journal* a series of compromising documents. Cited by *Le Monde* (28 October 2021), Haugen explained that Facebook's research had determined that content that 'polarizes, divides, or incites hatred results in greater commitment', and that the firm deliberately exploited this fact. She also showed that Facebook's managers were fully aware of the psychic disorders created by its subsidiary Instagram among adolescents less than 13 years old, and who felt ill at ease. But they targeted them anyway.[4] There has been a small victory for Frances Haugen: for the moment, Facebook has suspended its Instagram facility for users under 13 years of age.

A number of impressive works show the cognitive consequences of this phenomenon. Thus, an experimental study tested the impact of a smartphone on a group that earlier did not have access to one. In less than three months, it registered a very clear decline in their ability to pay attention, and they also received lower scores on tests in arithmetic. Their 'impulsiveness' increased in almost mechanical proportion to the time spent on their smartphones. A symmetrical study conducted by a group at Stanford disactivated access to Facebook for a month. The time freed up made it possible to see one's family and friends more, but also to watch more television ... Ultimately, the improvement in the well-being of the people tested was significant, to the point that, once the experiment was over, their digital consumption remained considerably lower. According to the study, one month without Facebook reduced anxiety and symptoms of depression by a quantity equivalent, in terms of well-being, to a gain of $30,000![5]

As in the case of tobacco, the risk of addiction to social networks is well established. The difference is that tobacco appeared to be the enemy of a society that was putting increasing emphasis on the body and health. Conversely, digital society immerses its participants in a virtual world, as in the film *Matrix*, to the point that nothing enables us to distinguish the real from the simulacrum. It destroys its users' critical defences by depriving them of the distance necessary to put into perspective the emotions that it elicits. A 'digital disinhibition' similar to that produced by drugs or alcohol is at work on social networks, where people allow themselves to depart at will from the norms of ordinary social life.[6] As Nathalie Heinich puts it so well, social networks stimulate competition to attract attention and 'induce people, by provocation, exaggeration, to say the unsayable, to display the unrepresentable. This extremist one-upmanship elicits powerful emotional responses that are immediately expressed by "likes" or "retweets" and automatically amplified by technology, without mediation, distancing, or hesitation.'

In the words of psychoanalyst Serge Tisseron, 'overexposed intimacy threatens the construction of a self' through the constant desire to display oneself advantageously, in a wild competition with others driven by a pathological quest for recognition. The compulsion that moves everyone to exhibit his or her private life leads to a profoundly deformed image of oneself. In the case of young children, overexposure to screens perturbs their ability to enter into relationships with others. Virtual reality distances them from a sensible perception of the physical world and the social environment: the real becomes dull and flat.[7]

Just fucking

Eva Illouz has analysed the transformation that the digital world imposes, on our love life in a way that admirably sheds light on the transformation of our sensibility.[8] Several hundreds of millions of people, she writes, have used 'their telephones as a sort of singles club open 24/7'. Bourgeois society had its bordellos to channel the libido, of which morality disapproved. Digital society throws open the windows of these virtual whorehouses where sexuality runs wild. One-third of the time spent on the Internet is devoted to pornography. An investigation conducted by the French Institute of Public Opinion (IFOP) found that 63 per cent of boys and 37 per cent of girls have visited pornographic sites. For young people, it is the whole relationship to sexuality that is disturbed, subsequently making it very difficult for these adolescents to have a love life that is respectful of others. According to a documentary broadcast on the French television channel M6, '44 percent of teenagers who have had sexual relations say that they reproduced practices that they had seen in porno films. The girls feel "obliged" to do certain things, to adopt certain sexual positions, and boys think that they absolutely must ask them to do so.'[9]

Illouz examines Tinder as the matrix of this new sexuality. She analyses it as the means of reducing love to 'just fucking', without any time 'lost' going through courtship rituals, without any affective management of the consequences of the sexual relationship. The 'one-night stand' is certainly not very original in human history, but what is new is the place that it now occupies in the imagination of adolescents. As one person questioned by Illouz puts it, sexuality in the digital age doesn't bother with having to deal with 'the other person's affective baggage'. In *A Lover's Discourse*, Roland Barthes magnificently illustrated the way in which this worry feeds erotic passion. Is he going to call me back? Was I rude? It's this ontological anxiety that Tinder eliminates. Sex with no future creates a psychic state in which each of the two parties believes he/she is in complete control, with no dependency on the other – just about the opposite of what a love relationship implies. By radically distinguishing sex from the feeling of love, digital sexuality causes the loss of the ability to recognize the other as a whole, as body and mind, in a relation in which each person expects the beloved to open the doors to a life to be invented.

Love as Tinder understands it elicits an existential void that the person concerned has to fill by multiplying encounters in a headlong rush that is perfectly representative of the addictive behaviours society provokes. Online sexuality organizes a tremendous contest that is not very different from the one that can be observed in the rest of the economy. Dating sites achieve the sexual neo-liberalism that Michel Houellebecq described in his first book, *Extension du domaine de la lutte*. In it, he reduced life in society, in a very Darwinian way, to the organization of an immense battle to find a partner.

It is in the deepest part of our lives, in our feelings of love, that this ultraliberal ideology seems to have found, thanks to Tinder, one of its most significant fulfilments.

Surveillance Capitalism

Another very impressive episode of *Black Mirror* is the one that tells the story of a girl obsessed by her social ranking, measured by the number of stars awarded to her by her friends or colleagues, in the way Uber drivers or Airbnb hosts are graded. In this series, everyone you meet can show agreement or disapproval with regard to you, with regard to the joy or sadness that you inspire, by giving you a good or a bad grade. A 'good' life is one that makes it possible to win the maximum of stars, the latter having in practice replaced money, which has the same objective of situating people in the social space. In this fantastic adventure, the young heroine wants to be invited to the marriage of a very highly graded friend from whom she hopes to receive the maximum number of points. But nothing happens as foreseen. A series of misadventures – a plane missed, a broken-down car, and the anger that ensues – cause her to lose all of her stars, ending up in prison. Then she abandons all oratorical precautions and insults her cellmate, drawing on an uncouth vocabulary of which no one would have thought her capable. By her face and her attitude, however, we understand that an immense relief is at work: she is free.

The manner in which the character in this episode subjects herself to the tyranny of ranking is the fictionalized form of a process of general surveillance that is in fact being established on the Web. At the same time that individuals are 'cretinized' by the customs of social networks, the system as a whole manages social life in a perfectly rational way. In China, a 'citizen score' already grades people, whether concerning their car accidents, failure to show up for work, alcohol consumption, late payments on loans, or, 'of course', their blog posts.[10] Democratic countries that believe they are not in danger of such an algorithmic dicta-torship are wrong. Thanks to face-recognition software, all your movements can now be traced. Soon it will no longer be necessary to validate a transportation ticket; a multi-functional chip installed in your body will take care of that. Despite all the precautions that are beginning to be taken regarding the use of data, it will be very difficult to prevent an operator from offering you advantageous bank loans or a job in return for the information about you that has been collected.

One can't help thinking of Orwell's famous book *1984*. In this novel, society is put under surveillance in order to avoid any dissent, while at the same time foreseeing periods during which cries of hatred will be permitted. We are experiencing Orwell's prophecy in a totally unexpected way. It is private consortiums that are monitoring individuals. However, in the GAFA[11] version of Big Brother, the goal is not to silence people but, on the contrary, to urge them to reveal their desires, their needs, their propensity to consume. Everything is logged, from the attention given to a television programme to the way a car is driven. In life according to GAFA, the 'private self' is lost. One's house is connected, allowing a mass of potential suppliers to enter the heart of family life.

Googlenomics

In a fundamental book, *The Age of Surveillance Capitalism: The Fight for a Human Future at the New Frontier of Power*, Shoshana Zuboff recounts GAFA's seizure of control over society. She offers a fascinating comparison between Henry Ford and the founder of Apple, Steve Jobs. Ford made a 'discovery' that was to revolutionize the industrial world. Walking through Chicago's slaughterhouses, he had a brilliant idea. The way pieces of meat were moved to be cut up by a butcher who remained immobile let him understand the principle that he was to apply to mass production where all cars are black. A similar revolution occurred with Apple. When Steve Jobs put the iPod on sale in October 2003, he turned the music industry upside down. The latter had been functioning on Ford's model. Mounting immense sales campaigns, the big labels told the consumer which artists to buy. Jobs made himself the proponent of a new modernity, opening an unlimited choice to customers.

The revolution brought about by Jobs and Ford is also found in the innovations in pricing they introduced. Ford had to fight his workers' chronic absenteeism, which amounted to a mute revolt against the staggering dehumanization of assembly-line work. His method, which was to launch what was called 'Fordism', consisted in doubling their salary to give them a stake in their work, thus creating another loop in which salary increases led to increases in productivity, which retroactively increased salaries. In a way that was just as revolutionary, it quickly became apparent to Jobs that the idea of selling songs by the unit, as in the first versions of iTunes, was an economic heresy when it would cost the company nothing to sell a hundred or a thousand songs for the same price. Stung by the pirating that was developing on the black market, digital companies were all to adopt a new model: streaming. Nothing belongs to the user, but his right to use is unlimited for a fixed subscription price. That is what the economist Jeremy Rifkin has called 'the age of access'. It is no longer objects, even if they are dematerialized, that are purchased, but membership in a community, a virtual club where all your desires are fulfilled.

However, GAFA's real innovation relative to Fordism took place in another register, in what Shoshana Zuboff calls the passage from a capitalism based on the extraction of surplus value to a different kind of capitalism based on the extraction of data. Zuboff reminds us of the distant time when the founders of Google, Larry Page and Sergei Brin, declared that they detested advertising. When the firm was established in 1998, they didn't want to do anything that would compromise the credibility of their search engine. At that time, Google was thinking of renting its services to a few companies such as Yahoo! The rupture came when they understood that they were sitting on a gold mine: one that procured information about users, what is called UPI, 'user profile information'. This turning point marked the transformation of young libertarians into ultra-capitalists showing no respect for their customers.

'Googlenomics' was conceived by an economist, Hal Varian. A respected professor at Berkeley whose introduction to microeconomics has been read by several million students, Varian was recruited by Google in 2002. He explained to the founders of the firm how new theories of auctioning that were very fashionable among economists could be applied to advertising online. Inspired by him, Ad Words, Google's new advertising agency, was a triumph. Renamed Ad Sense in 2010, the firm's revenues exploded. The search engine did not serve solely to make advertising 'passive'. It charged firms a kind of 'revolutionary tax' to appear at the head of the recommendations given to users. As one producer put it, appearing on page 2 of Google amounted to a sure digital death.

Facebook, created the year that Google was listed on the stock market, immediately understood how to get rich as well. Sheryl Sandberg, who had created Ad Words, was poached by Mark Zuckerberg's firm to make it another giant of online advertising. For Zuboff, this was the moment when the 'extraction of data' regarding consumers replaced the 'extraction of plus-value' from workers. Everything is done to enter users' private worlds. The two firms joined to engage in ferocious lobbying to avoid regulation of data capturing. They also succeeded in convincing the competition authorities to allow them to buy their rivals. Thus, Google bought YouTube for $1.65 billion. At the time it was acquired, YouTube had barely sixty-five employees, the majority of whom were highly qualified engineers. That is equivalent to a valuation of more than $25 million per employee. In April 2012, Facebook bought Instagram for

$1 billion. The company then had thirteen employees. That represents about $77 million per worker. In 2014, Facebook bought WhatsApp for $19 billion. At that time, WhatsApp employed fifty-five people, which yields an evaluation of $345 million per employee!

We can only be amazed to see so much intelligence, so much knowledge, put in the service of a single objective, derisory in view of the means that AI is capable of offering: online advertising! One wants to believe that there are other uses. Concerning GAFAs themselves, it is clear that their terrain will not remain confined forever. Facebook tried to create its own currency, the Libra, competing not only with traditional banks but also with the sovereign power of central banks. The experiment has temporarily failed (it survives under a different name, the Diem), but it cannot fail to resurface in one manner or another. In the meantime, Facebook is migrating towards the metaverse, the 'meta-universe', where it would like to see whole areas of social life settled: public or professional meetings, life-sized games, imaginary journeys, etc. An immense transformation is being prepared that cannot be reduced to merely 'cretinizing' human beings, but in which everything remains to be thought through. It took time for the printing press to produce all its effects – among other reasons, because the great majority of the population was illiterate when Gutenberg printed his first Bible.

3

Waiting for the Robots

The Death of Kings

The quarantine during the Covid epidemic caused people to discover the immense potential contained within new technologies. Work from home suddenly appeared, for at least a third of employees, to be an immediately practicable option. Remote medicine took off when it was noticed that the relation between patient and caregiver did not require the systematic presence of the patient in the doctor's office. A new way of conceiving the productive world sprang up, very different from earlier practices. Meeting face to face with one's colleagues or one's clients became one option among others.

To understand this astonishing complicity between the appearance of the virus and digital capitalism, we have to return briefly to the past. In 1948, the French economist Jean Fourastié proposed an analysis of economic transformations that provides a key that is essential for understanding the mutation that Covid has accelerated. Fourastié declared that the 'great hope of the twentieth century' was the transition from an industrial society to a service society. Human beings, he explained, had cultivated the land for millennia, and then industrial matter during the last two centuries. In the service society whose blooming was heralded by Fourastié, humans themselves were what was going to be cultivated. His great hope was that the economy would finally succeed in humanizing itself in a world in which everyone would look after one another, as coach, educator, or caregiver. Faced with this excellent news, Fourastié nonetheless pointed to a 'problem' that, in his view, was not really a problem: this service economy would give rise to much slower economic growth. If the product I'm selling is the time that I spend with my client, as does a nurse or an educator, then the economy must stagnate unless we work more to earn more.

In a splendid book, *Performing Arts: The Economic Dilemma*, William Baumol and William Bowen indirectly expanded on Fourastié's intuitions based on an eloquent example, that of *performing arts*. Their starting point is a simple observation: it takes just as long to act a play by Shakespeare as it did on the day of its first performance. Time depends on the actors' words: Richard II hears the 'sad stories of the death of kings' at the same immutable speed. But since it is deprived of 'gains in productivity', the theatre has become increasingly expensive relative to other sectors of the economy – those that use the new techniques to reduce the amount of work-time required for their production. This 'cost disease' constantly reappears, making it expensive to produce ballets and operas because they lack any lever that would allow them to generate gains in productivity. Thus, the New York Philharmonic Orchestra saw its costs multiply five-fold over a century, after taking inflation into account. That is what explains why theatre attendance regularly decreases, and why artists have a hard time making a living. They frequently have jobs in another sphere of work, usually teaching, and, despite the stars' salaries, their rank in the scale of incomes has difficulty remaining at the middle level.

This pathology can be summed up in a comparison: *objects* cost less and less, and it is the *human being* who becomes the most expensive commodity, and all the more because humans have to meet in groups in the same place. For example, today it is much more expensive to go to the theatre than to buy a Bible, whereas in Shakespeare's time the reverse was true. This observation applies to all the live arts. That is why it is now much more expensive to hire a troupe of actors and rent a performance hall in the city centre that can accommodate a large audience; why everything costs more in a sector, such as the theatre, where human beings are the main 'raw material'. That was Baumol and Bowen's unanswerable conclusion at the end of their analysis. It provoked a shock and made the American government more aware of the need to give greater importance to public subsidies of culture. But that did not prevent the 'natural' course of history from occurring. Live theatre has been cannibalized by radio, television, and now Netflix and other online platforms, all media that have made it possible for the actor who tells 'sad stories of the death of kings' to be heard as many times as possible by an audience that grows steadily larger, without having to move.

The current revolution may be said to offer a solution of the same kind to the service society as a whole. We're talking about human beings, as Fourastié said. But human beings whose relations to one another are now 'optimized' as much as possible.

The Industrialization of Services

Services: they can be defined as the whole of the activities in which the buyer and the supplier have to meet for production to take place. A barber has to cut his customer's hair 'in person', just as a theatre actor has to play his role in front of an audience. 'The industrialization of services' is an expression that is a priori self-contradictory but it allows us to designate the process of rationalization that seeks to reduce the cost of this interaction as much as possible. There are several methods. Television is an example of a technology that multiplies the number of a supplier's customers. This is called achieving 'economies of scale'. But there are other methods: for example, the supplier can be replaced by an algorithm that lets the customer figure out by himself what to do. That is what happens when you have to manage, without an assistant, your online reservations or your bank accounts. A third method is the one proposed by tele-medicine. There is still a supplier and a customer, face to face, but not necessarily in the same place. Only indispensable meetings are retained. The central question is, obviously, how what is 'indispensable' is determined. Esther Duflo, in her book *Good Economics for Hard Times: Better Answers to Our Biggest Problems*, co-written with Abhijit Banerjee, gives a troubling example of the algorithmic revolution: that of her sister, the director of an NGO, who has no human assistant. The IBM computer Watson takes care of all the tasks ordinarily entrusted to an assistant: making her appointments, gathering accounting data, etc. As the economist Kathryn Shaw emphasizes in this regard, those who are sometimes called 'knowledge workers' actually spend a great deal of time doing things not at the heart of their trade. According to her estimate, 60 per cent of a researcher's time, for example, is diverted from his/her research to deal with administrative tasks. The stage that is looming with AI is one in which the algorithm will be able to take initiatives: reserving your hotel room when it has noted that you have an appointment in another city, offering reports on meetings in which you have participated, communicating with other machines to prepare a professional meeting, etc.

Another example is that of call centres. Most of these have been relocated in poor countries that operate in India for English speakers or in North Africa for French speakers. The precise codification of these tasks, entrusted to people who have no knowledge of the questions that they are asked, was possible because of a so-called 'Pareto principle', according to which the range of questions asked is in fact very limited. For instance, if the question most frequently asked represents 50 per cent of the total, the second will be 25 per cent, the third 12.5 percent, and so on. Here, three questions cover 85 per cent of the cases concerned. It is this work of codification that used to make it possible to relocate call centres to foreign countries, and that today allows a computer to take the place of a human being.

That is why we spend an incalculable amount of time pressing 1, 2, or 3 to obtain the answer from a machine (my TV is broken, what should I do?) before reaching the holy grail of a human being, who will come in only as a last resort. And even then, the person who answers you will often repeat the same digitized protocol before it refers you, if it is absolutely necessary, to a real technician. Emotional dialogue is one of the challenges that remains to be met. According to Laurence Devillers, the recognition of affects and their stimulation, using clues drawn from the voice, face, and gestures, is the current stage of the development of what are also called 'chatbots', or conversational agents.[1]

Medicine is also directly affected. Medical algorithms are capable of extracting from a virtually infinite library of data and articles the elements pertinent to the analysis of this or that symptom. Dermatologists already know how to make use of the millions of images that have been analysed and diagnosed, which permits them to find appropriate references immediately. Here it is especially a matter of an aid to diagnosis; for the moment, no one is thinking about replacing a doctor by an algorithm. Radiologists are in greater danger. Their trade consists of taking X-rays and interpreting them for their colleagues. AI will be able to carry out this initial diagnosis by itself, the physician who ordered it being responsible for consulting a few specialists who have survived the digital purge if he deems that necessary.

Self-medication is another field that is thriving, even if it is on the margin of legality. You have a slight temperature and a sore throat: a digital licensed practice nurse reassures you and advises you to drink a nice warm grog and take two aspirin tablets. If you're still feeling ill the next day, go see a doctor. The good news is that these algorithms will also serve to redefine the jobs of practice nurses, who will become efficient intermediaries between the patient and the doctor.

The industrialization of services also imitates the process of rationalization that we observe in factories, except that here it's the consumer who is directly 'Taylorized'. Shopping centres without staff are already in place, particularly so they can be open on Sundays. You enter, select what you want, and leave. Facial recognition mechanisms make it possible to identify you, debiting your credit card, which you have registered in advance (one can imagine that you will have the option to validate, if you really want to, the expenditures that are billed to your bank account). The idea of entering a completely dehumanized shopping centre makes a chill run down one's back, but Amazon has already put the next step in place, eliminating the need to move physically.

The self-driving car

Being driven around by an algorithm has not yet entered our mores, but the time is coming. Almost twenty years have elapsed since, under the aegis of the DARPA (Defence Advanced Research Projects Agency), some fifteen self-driving vehicles tried to travel 20 kilometres, leaving from the city of Barstow, California, at the heart of the Mojave Desert.[2] None of these vehicles succeeded in doing so, most of them stopping a few kilometres from the starting line. One year later, on 8 October 2005, the results were much more convincing. The route included about a hundred curves, three tunnels, and a mountain pass. A Volkswagen, transformed by Sebastian Thrun of Stanford University, won the race at the end of an epic 7 hours. Google quickly put itself in the vanguard of research by poaching, in 2008, Thrun and his team. The result was up to the occasion: in 2012, the Google fleet travelled 30,000 miles without accidents on motorways connecting great metropolises and in the latter's traffic jams. The success of autonomous vehicles subsequently continued to grow, leading to the triumph of Tesla, which makes 100 per cent electric cars and is run by Elon Musk, who is also known for his space shuttles.

The progress of the autonomous vehicle is obvious, and yet it remains difficult to allow the security of passengers to be entrusted to an algorithm whose slightest flaw might cost them their lives. Even if the risks are statistically lower than for a human driver, it is clear that we do not use the same criteria to judge the reliability of a bus driver and that of an algorithm. A machine that hits a pedestrian who ignored a red light will be judged far more severely than a human. In fact, people will not be truly at ease with autonomous vehicles until those driven by humans have been prohibited. As soon as they have reached a monopoly on urban traffic, they will be able to communicate with each other easily and avoid accidents and traffic jams. That will be the end of the pleasure of driving, and some people will not resign themselves to it, but such is modern life.

The Thinking Robot

The fantasy of anthropomorphic robots is winning a larger place in the contemporary imagination. Gill Pratt has drawn an analogy with the development of vision, 500 million years ago. Sight helped to launch the multiplication of living

species on Earth.[3] Robots may be reaching this stage. The
rate of error in labelling the content of photos had fallen
from 30 per cent in 2010 to less than 5 per cent in 2016,
and is now below humans' threshold of error. Progress in
voice recognition is just as spectacular. Apple's Siri, Google
Assistant, and Amazon's Alexa rely on new interfaces to
recognize the words pronounced, interpret their meaning,
and reply accordingly. Pratt also stresses the fact that digital
machines have the revolutionary ability to instantaneously
share their knowledge among themselves.

On the strength of these advances, researchers are working
on robots that are soft to the touch, thus giving a pleasant
feeling to their interactions with humans.[4] Japan is at
the forefront in all these areas due to its rapidly ageing
population. It is a country hermetically sealed against
immigration, whereas in most others (notably, the United
States), the latter provides a labour force – often poorly
paid and easily exploited – that cares for dependent people.
That is in fact the debate that is hidden behind the one on
immigration: to stop immigration is to accelerate the roboti-
zation of care for the aged. The booming sector of home
automation is preparing for this by computerizing the homes
of the elderly with sensors to monitor the state of their
health, and their possible falls. The presence of robots in the
apartments of old or dependent people is also supposed to
allow caregivers to monitor their patients remotely in order
to perform simple acts such as administering their medicines,
taking their temperature, or simply to provide medical
personnel an overall field of vision as soon as the robot can
accompany the patient into the remote corners of his/her life.

Recruit and judge

The use of AI for hiring procedures or recruitment is already
being generalized. Universities use algorithms to evaluate

candidates for admission, taking into account the schools they have attended, and perhaps awarding a bonus to those who emphasize their para-academic activities. The stage that is already under way in the private sector uses an algorithm to interview job applicants, judging both the content and the form of their performance: the ease with which the applicant speaks, smiles, and shows empathy. Recruiting software used to track candidatures has formed partnerships with most of the professional sites such as Linkedin or Monster.com. Soon, you will be automatically contacted by recruiters, without having to do anything at all, other than have a brightly coloured CV and a video that will make it possible to evaluate you.

In the film *Elysium*, a dystopia embodied on the screen by Matt Damon and Jodie Foster, algorithms go farther: policing and justice are entrusted to robots The robot-judge calculates the probabilities that they will commit another offence and sets a corresponding punishment. The robot offers Damon the option of appealing to a human, a proposal that he nonetheless rejects, for fear that the punishment might be more severe. This is only science fiction, but the book *Noise*, written by Kahneman and his co-authors,[5] presents a very rigorous argument that can be interpreted as a plea for an algorithmic justice system! The point of departure of their analysis is the implacable demonstration of the fallibility of human judgement. Judges are as contaminated by their moods as other humans are. An analysis of several thousand judicial decisions has shown that they make more severe decisions on the Mondays that follow the local football team's defeat! In France, an equally exhaustive study has shown that judges are more clement if it is the accused's birthday (Kahneman adding maliciously that the hypothesis that they are also more clement on their own birthdays was not tested). Juries are also victims of false statistical theories. For example, they are less likely to grant asylum to a migrant if they have already granted it to two preceding applicants.

Judges are also very sensitive to the temperature outside. Several studies on hundreds of thousands of cases have shown that sentences are more severe on very hot days. The influence of fine weather on the stock market has also been analysed: the market rises when the sun shines (as long as it's not too hot, no doubt). A study cited by Kahneman showed that examination boards in universities did not escape this influence of the weather. When weather is average, the examiners are very attentive to the academic quality of the files: grades, the quality of term papers. When the weather is good, on the other hand, they are more sensitive to the non-academic qualities of the candidates ... Physicians are just as vulnerable. After a long workday, they have a much stronger propensity to prescribe opiates than they do at the beginning of the day, as if their own fatigue were applied to the patients they are examining.

Compared with these errors in judgement, algorithms offer an alternative that will not depend on either the time spent on the task or the outside temperature. A team of researchers directed by Sendhil Mullainatham of MIT trained AI to simulate judges' ability to predict whether another crime will be committed by the defendant. The team had access to the same information as the judges concerning, notably, the delinquent's previous offences. To avoid any stereotyped judgement, no data regarding gender or race was provided to the computer. Relative to humans, AI significantly improved the quality of the judgements. Releases on bail granted by AI would have reduced the rate of criminality by almost 25 per cent, with a constant rate of incarceration. The MIT researchers also showed that this rate of incarceration could be reduced by 40 per cent for a given recidivism objective. As soon as the objective (here, reducing the average rate of recidivism) is easy to state in statistical terms, AI wins unambiguously.

After this long demonstration in favour of AI, Kahneman and his co-authors nonetheless warn against the virtues of the latter. The fantasies of a film like *Minority Report*, inspired by a famous science fiction novel, suggest that there could be, over our heads, a science that would have the means to predict human behaviours perfectly. Even in simple cases in which it is a question of predicting heart attacks, AI certainly does better than the doctors, but the final result remains mediocre. In fact, physicians err because the 'objective' ability to predict heart attacks is weak, more than because of their own limitations. The problem is just as much in the denial that grips experts as it is in the contrary accusation of ignorance that is made against them.

A digital morality?

The development of self-driving cars has forced car manufacturers to consider moral problems for which they were not prepared. The question is this: if the self-driving vehicle is confronted with the dilemma of deciding whether to run over a pedestrian to avoid running over two others, what will it do? Will it take into account the fact that the pedestrian in danger is young and the other two are old? Will it consider the fact that the pedestrian threatened has a right to be on the crosswalk? These questions, which amuse us or frighten us, are only beginning. They do not frighten theorists of the algorithm, because they prepare us for the world the theorists have in mind: a society in which a growing number of decisions, including those involving caregiving or judging, will be made by machines.

As Martin Gibert shows humorously in his book *Faire la morale aux robots*, these debates often take as their point of

departure a dilemma analysed by the philosopher Philippa
Foot in 1967: the tramway dilemma. Imagine a tram speeding
along that might kill five people at once if it is not diverted in
some way. A switch would make it possible to divert it onto
another track, but on it there is another railway worker who
is just as innocent and who would be doomed to die. What
to do? To answer that question, MIT created a website,
'the Moral Machine Experiment', which allows us to test
the morality people prefer, depending on their age, gender,
and education. On average, people prefer to save the most
people possible, and the young ones first of all. However,
sometimes (in countries in Asia and the Middle East, for
example), it is the elderly individuals that they want to save.
This spontaneous morality is called 'utilitarian'. Its founda-
tions were laid in the eighteenth century by Jeremy Bentham.
It holds that an action is morally justified if it increases the
pleasures of the people concerned. Saving five people while
killing one is for Bentham a desirable, moral action. But
a true utilitarian will be more specific: if there are five old
men on the one hand, and one young man or young woman
on the other, the precise calculation might be different ... It
is this morality that economists most often favour. It leads
to macabre calculations concerning the 'value' of a human
life (in France, the figure is 3 million euros) that would
make it possible to decide whether expensive works on a
railway track are justified or not. It is the particular case of
a morality called 'consequentialist', which judges the value
of an act by its consequences.

Kant's moral philosophy is often opposed to Bentham's
as its counterpoint. Kant deduces the morality of an action
from the principles that guide it, rather than by considering
its effects. This morality, called 'deontological', posits that
there are absolute principles that have to be respected in
all circumstances: for example, not to torture anyone. One
way of understanding what it would imply in the case of the

tramway is to follow the thought experiment proposed by another American philosopher, Judith Jarvis Thomson. In her example, the five endangered people can no longer be saved by moving the switch but one can do it by pushing onto the rails a random individual whose fall would cause the train to go off the rails and thus avoid hitting the five innocents. Supposing that the person who had to make the decision was herself too small for her self-sacrifice to have the intended effect, must she deliberately push onto the tracks the more corpulent man who is standing beside her? Most of the people asked this question would generally be opposed to the suggestion, even if, in the case of the switch, they were able to reply in the positive. They have moved from a utilitarian morality to a 'deontological' morality. From this new moral point of view, we can no longer dispose of someone else's life (let's say, without his/her consent), even if it is to save five times as many. There is a higher principle, the absolute respect for the 'dignity' of each person, which challenges the right to make him/her a means to an end.

Which morality should be chosen for driving assisted by a computer? There is a third way, Gibert explains, which is that of 'virtue'. It is no longer a question of setting utilitarian or Kantian parameters, but rather of behaving as a virtuous person would in a similar situation. Aristotle called this 'prudence' (*phronesis*, practical reason) – namely, the ability to act in the right way at the right time. How would the wise man reply to a child who believes in Santa Claus: would he leave him his illusions (his well-being, following the utilitarian approach), or would he teach him the truth (in accord with the Kantian appeal to principles)? The wise philosopher would know. You'd like your car to be driven the way Martin Luther King or Nelson Mandela would have driven it? How can you gather the data that would enable you to grasp the way these wise figures would make decisions in unforeseeable situations? It will not be enough to replace the word 'car' with 'carriage' or 'horse' to extrapolate what they would have done.

The Stake of the Century

'A troubling passion drives the human being: engendering artificial doubles of himself, like God creating humans in his own image',[6] writes Éric Sadin. The latter is one of the foremost experts on AI, which he describes as an 'alethetic power' – *alethia* meaning 'truth' in Greek. The new anthropomorphic age of technology is very different from the one that consisted in giving humans a lever to increase their power of action. AI does much more than organize an efficient relation between humans and matter: it substitutes itself for humans to grasp the real, the machine now being 'considered more reliable than we are'. Historically, he adds, norms, conventions, and prejudices were forged in a multitude of places: nothing is more urgent than to keep alive the institutions in which social life is elaborated, whether they are schools, parliaments, or law courts. This is the stake of the century.

In reality, replacing humans with algorithms is anything but simple – and that could be considered fortunate. A survey of 3,000 leaders conducted by the McKinsey Global Institute has revealed that the adoption of AI outside the technology sector remains embryonic. There are still many obstacles to be cleared before a robot replaces a human being. Robots lack the 'common sense' Le Cun talked about. Distinguishing a dirty flower pot that has to be cleaned from another pot that contains a plant is easy for a human. Robots still have trouble doing the same. There are single-purpose robots that are capable of carrying out specific tasks, such as cleaning floors, but there is still no polyvalent model capable, for example, of detecting and eliminating rubbish.

Robots are really at ease only in specific spaces such as factories or depots where everything is marked out for them.

The limit cases of factories entirely governed by algorithms are still completely fantastical. An example of this disappointment is that of Elon Musk. In 2016, he announced that the new Tesla Model 3 would be built in an entirely automated way. Its code name, 'Alien Dreadnought', intentionally connoted science fiction. Very advanced technologies, far beyond current practices, were used. The complete automatization of work was supposed to make it possible to increase the speed of production. The raw materials would go in at one end, and cars would emerge at the other, and between them robots would do everything at a very rapid velocity. The factory, which was supposed to be totally operational by the end of 2018, wasn't. In the middle of 2018, it became clear that production was creating problems that could not be resolved. The operation was described as a hell, 'a few weeks from catastrophe'. Total automation was a mistake. 'Humans are underrated', was Musk's sibylline conclusion on Twitter. In an interview published in *L'Usine nouvelle*, Alain Supiot denounced the 'fantasy of putting human affairs under automatic guidance'.[7]

It takes time for a new technology to find its place. IBM's Watson may be a formidable instrument, capable of replacing humans for many administrative tasks, but few people would have the temerity to entrust to it the responsibility – a priori simple – for paying their bills. Electricity is a classic example that testifies to the time that can separate the discovery of a new technology and its full utilization. The economist Paul David showed that in 1919 half of American companies were still not using electricity, thirty years after the discovery of alternating current. Electricity ended up illuminating cities and then apartments, which was a direct gain in itself. But its full use depended on many other subsequent applications – radio, television, the washing machine – that were invented later. The peculiar feature of a paradigm-breaking technology is to offer a set of possibilities that go beyond the understanding of its inventors. The steam engine was initially used to pump water out of mines, and it took several decades before people understood that it would allow railways to move thousands of passengers from one place to another. The errors made by the inventors themselves regarding the utility of their discoveries are legion. Edison thought that his phonograph would serve to record the last will and testament of dying people. Bell thought that the telephone would be used to listen to a concert played in a distant place!

The current uncertainty regarding the possible uses of AI is good news and bad news. Good, because nothing is determined in advance. Bad, because we don't know where we're going. A law named after Roy Amara, the former president of the Palo Alto Institute for the Future, explains that we have a tendency to exaggerate the short-term impacts of new technologies, whereas we underestimate their long-term effects. If nothing momentous will probably happen in the next five or six years, what about a (somewhat) longer time? Traffic in cities, the management of bank accounts, and healthcare will probably move into the field of algorithmic science. But many other domains will also be transformed: the brain–machine interface, life in the metaverse ... What seems to be written in advance is that the digital revolution is going to reconfigure social life profoundly. Everyone will be asked to reflect on the way to replace human collaborators with algorithmic assistants, to organize a drastic reduction of face-to-face meetings, radically upsetting our relationships to others. It is this major risk of losing social links that is already turning our societies upside down, bringing with it an incalculable batch of psychological and social harms.

4

Political Anomie

Impoverishing Growth

The digital revolution is supposed to improve the conditions of existence in advanced societies. However, it offers the paradox of an 'impoverishing' technology. In the United States, where it was born, a worker's wages have remained practically the same for the past fifty years.[1] This stagnation is accompanied by an explosion of the remuneration of the wealthiest. The works of Thomas Piketty and his co-authors have shown that the lower half of the population saw its share of the national revenue collapse, passing in half a century from 20% to 10% of the total. During this same time, the richest 1% followed the exactly opposite path: its share rose from 10% to 20%! This increase in inequalities in the United States contrasts spectacularly with the post-war years, when the growth of purchasing power was almost identical at all levels of society.

The digital revolution follows two great industrial periods: that of electricity in the twentieth century and that of the steam engine in the century before that. These two revolutions had considerable impacts on society, but they were

very different from one another. The electric revolution
gave rise to the large assembly lines whose effect was to
make social relations denser, and to give a new power to
labour unions. The first industrial revolution, that of the
steam engine, had itself created the great modern factories
(the 'factory system'), but its social impact was much more
brutal. Peasants had to leave their original communities and
go to the city to form an immense 'industrial reserve army',
to use Marx's expression. For more than half a century, the
situation of the British working classes constantly deterio-
rated.[2] The wages of weavers continued to fall in the measure
that they were replaced by machines, and this decrease
ceased only when they had completely disappeared. In his
work on the condition of the working class in England,
published in 1845, Engels, Marx's co-author, worried about
this 'situation of the working class, that is, the immense
majority of people. What will happen to these millions of
human beings who possess nothing, who consume today
what they earned yesterday?'

The contradiction between the rise of technologies that
we would like to think are always favourable to economic
progress, on the one hand, and the impoverishment of the
popular classes in the nineteenth century, on the other
hand, has never ceased to trouble economists. Robert Allen
has spoken of 'Engels' pause', referring to the passage
quoted above, to characterize this explosion of poverty
amid a world reputed to be more productive. The main
origin of contemporary social disorder, particularly in
the United States, is Reagan's free-market revolution. Its
target was the bargaining power of labour unions. The
latter have always played an important role in matters of
wage equity, pushing for a form of internal redistribution
to the benefit of the lowest ranks of the social hierarchy.
By proceeding to externalize tasks that require the least
skill, companies have wrecked that aspiration. In his thesis,

Philippe Askenazy has shown that the first firms to be restructured or 're-engineered' were often the most union-ized.[3] In the new productive world that was established in the 1980s, technologies of information and communication came after the event, so to speak: they made possible an organization of work in which tasks are delegated to firms that are always farther away. The fax machine was the first revolutionary instrument easing the transmission of data from one enterprise to another. Then, during the 1990s, with the Internet, the mutation was total.

In this new system, the best-performing firms become the operators of a mosaic of other enterprises to which the least profitable activities are delegated. The appearance of 'superstar' firms, whose content in terms of jobs is small, is the most visible expression of this transformation. This is the model whose archetype is GAFA, but it is in reality much more general. In each sector, the five best-performing enterprises have considerably increased their share of the market. With the exception of financial firms, they have far fewer employees than their competitors. Whatever sector we examine, the fewer employees a firm has, the more it succeeds. Economists call this 'scale without mass' an economics of scale without weight. Netflix or Google can double their bottom lines without having to double their personnel. What is surprising is that this model seems to be established everywhere, not only in the sector of digital industrialists. In the United States, the 100 leading enterprises used to produce a third of the overall added value. Today, their share has risen to 50 per cent.[4] It is these 'superstar' firms that contribute heavily to reducing the proportion of added value paid in wages.

Not all countries are affected equally by this revolution. France, for example, resists the decline of the share of wages in overall revenue. There is a good reason for this, and a bad reason. The bad one is that it does not have, like the United States, a great many enterprises on the frontier of technological mutations. The good reason is that its social institutions, such as the minimum wage or social protection in general, have allowed France better to resist the erosion of the remuneration of labour. Thus France has been less affected by the rise of inequalities, though it has not been entirely spared.[5]

However, France has been struck, like most of the advanced countries, by a general slowing of growth that has only become more evident, decade after decade. Everywhere, one can see a general loss of steam in productivity gains that is ultimately manifested, ineluctably, by a slowing of the rise in wages.[6] Household revenue, corrected for size, is no longer rising much at all, whereas in the 1960s it doubled every fifteen years. In France, as in the United States, the general cause of the slow-down is indissociable from the 'cost disease' that Baumol talked about: it is much more difficult to generate gains in productivity in a service society than it is in an industrial society. What is at stake for the algorithmic revolution is to 'solve' this problem, but the revolution is only just beginning, and from the point of view of the workers who suffer its effects, the remedy may be worse than the disease.

The major consequence of this already visible transformation of the productive system is the ongoing collapse of intermediary jobs. Everywhere in advanced countries, in France as in the United States, the share of such jobs has decreased.[7] 'Creative' jobs, which are at the very top of the social ladder, have been well rewarded. It is stock traders, football players, and producers of algorithms who are the great winners in the contemporary world. All those who can use digital techniques to increase, without limits, the size of their clientele have benefitted from the new world that is being put in place. At the other extreme, the bottom of the social ladder, it is the personal caregivers who have increased most in number, while at the same time remaining very poorly paid. This polarization between the two extremes actualizes the predicted logic of comparative advantages of humans over machines: sensitivity and creativity.

The most important political consequence of this process is the continuing erosion of the middle class, at least up until now. Administrative and commercial tasks whose role was to connect the high and the low levels of an enterprise have all receded, as if firms no longer needed jobs located in the middle of the hierarchy to function efficiently. For the middle classes as well as for the lower classes, which have been deprived of hope for the advancement that had been promised them, it is a theatre of immense disillusions that has risen up. The loss of confidence in themselves and in their social future is an extremely violent shock for the people concerned.

Working-Class Suicide

In their great book *Deaths of Despair*, the economists Anne Case and Angus Deaton told the story of the growing despair of the American working classes, caught between an industrial world that is vanishing and a digital world that has no place for them. In the nineteenth century, there was a famous report by Dr Villermé on the poverty of the French working classes, which warned against their psychic and physical exhaustion. Case and Deaton's book is the equivalent for the beginning of the twenty-first century. One of its authors, Angus Deaton, a Nobel Prize-winner in economics, had written a book entitled *The Great Escape: Health, Wealth, and the Origins of Inequality* (2013) which analysed the decline of death in the West thanks to the great medical inventions of the twentieth century: antibiotics, progress in the battle against rabies, cholera, etc. *Deaths of Despair* is a kind of despairing codicil to the preceding work. In the United States, what medicine gave, society has taken back.

The book is a dive into American traumas. It narrates the discovery of a brutal statistical fact – the increase in the mortality of a very precise social category: Whites, aged between 45 and 54, without a university degree. The term 'deaths of despair' used by Case and Deaton groups together suicide, drugs, and alcohol. Taken together, these deaths have tripled in less than thirty years. Deprived of a future, suffering the consequences of a growing social solitude, the American working classes fell into the trap of a frantic consumption of opiates, encouraged by unscrupulous pharmaceutical laboratories.

The rise of mortality in the course of recent decades was a totally unforeseen shock. The decline of morbidity among adults used to be one of the irresistible forces of the twentieth century, which neither the 1930s nor World War II hindered. Setting aside the Spanish flu of 1918, of which Covid is partly an echo, the tendency seems ineluctable. In the hidden epidemic represented by the consumption of opiates, the absence of a university degree was one of the most fundamental markers. Whites born in 1980 who did not hold a university degree registered a rate of suicide four times higher than the rest of the population.

The cases analysed by Case and Deaton are the visible portion of a more general phenomenon of abandonment experienced by the working classes. Yesterday's jobs offered workers a strong social bond, enabling them to truly be part of an enterprise like Ford or GM, of which they were proud. Daron Acemoglu has summed up the problem as being that of the disappearance of 'good jobs', positions that were well paid and accompanied by prospects of promotion.[8] The disappearance of the big industrial firms put an end to these possibilities of advancement. Beaud and Pialoux made the same observation about France: the possibility of social promotion offered to workers has disappeared. These days, a worker has almost no chance of becoming a manager.[9]

Post-industrial society has destroyed the structure of earlier occupational spaces. The obsession with external-izing everything has shifted maintenance men, drivers, sales reps, etc., towards independent firms offering the lowest possible salaries. Unskilled workers in service sectors are no longer immersed in the dense social relationships that used to characterize industrial companies. These same actors are over-represented in the Yellow Vests movement in France: drivers and nursing assistants are very present on rounda-bouts, whereas the labour union representatives have often been kept at a distance.

Return to Durkheim

To understand the causes of these deaths from despair, we have to return to Émile Durkheim and his book *Le Suicide*, published in 1897. This is a book of an exceptional subtlety, which founded French sociology and, more generally, the very possibility of a science of society. The fact that such a singular phenomenon as suicide manifests strong regularities, notably from one year to the next, shows that it obeys general laws that the sociologist can study. Durkheim takes great care to demon-strate that suicide is a phenomenon that is far more social than psychological in nature. For example, he notes that social groups that are over-represented in psychiatric hospitals are not the same ones that commit suicide. Women, for example, commit suicide much less often than men do, whereas they more often experience depression. Similarly, when we examine the figures by religious affiliation, we find that Jews seldom commit suicide, though they are proportionally more likely to spend time in mental health hospitals. What causes suicide is not the individual, but society. It is the loss of a link to the social world that leads people to take their own lives.

Durkheim begins by analysing what he calls 'egoistic suicide', which affects people that modernity has cut off

from their attachments. In the nineteenth century, the first
victims were peasants forced to abandon their lands to work
in a city. A century later, as Christian Baudelot and Roger
Establet show in updating these statistics, things are exactly
the other way round – it is in the countryside that suicides
are the most numerous, but the cause remains the same:
social solitude.[10]

In addition to social solitude, Durkheim stresses the role of
another factor, close to the first but different in scope, which he
calls 'social anomie', the feeling that society no longer obeys
known laws. When the order of the world becomes unintel-
ligible, the suicide rate rises. The most striking example, at
the time that Durkheim was writing, is that of divorce. It
deprives the people concerned of points of reference, of ways
of theorizing their place in the world. A state of disturbance,
agitation, and discontent results. Regions where divorce had
increased the fastest were also those where the suicide rate
rose the most. According to Durkheim, a divorced person
cannot project himself into the future.

Contemporary anomie

As Luc Rouban, a researcher at the CEVIPOF (Centre for
Research on Politics at Sciences Po), shows, it is in fact on
this terrain of social solitude that the French fractures are
the deepest.[11] To the question of whether France is a united
nation or one torn into communities, only 42 per cent of the
sample said it is united, while 53 per cent said that it is an
archipelago of communities, validating a book by Jérôme
Fourquet.[12] The economic prism itself plays a weak role: the
answers hardly vary whether the respondent is pro-market
or protectionist. A growing part of the population is infected
by this 'social anomie' that Durkheim speaks of – the feeling
of having lost one's membership in society, of no longer
understanding the role that one plays in it.

CEVIPOF questioned French people regarding their social ties in a very broad sense: 'Do you feel that you belong above all to the national community, to a community of people who share your values (religious or otherwise); to a community of people who speak the same language or who have the same geographical origins as you do; to a community of people who share the same tastes, the same way of life; or do you feel that you don't belong to any community?' Despite the very broad scope of the answers suggested, 45 per cent of the French said they did not belong to any community. This 'anomic' group is overwhelming in the working classes, in which 65 per cent of the respondents declare no membership, whereas this figure falls to 25 per cent among the upper classes.

Jérôme Fourquet and Jean-Laurent Cassely have written a fascinating book about workers' confusion, which shows the whole extent of the desocialization of which they are the victims.[13] They describe the transition from a world in which the factory was the beating heart of workers' identity, to another in which shopping centres play this role. As an emblematic example of this evolution, they note that on the day after the Yellow Vests' first demonstration, on 18 November 2018, a delegation decided to block access not to the prefecture, but to Disneyland, so that they could demand free admission. This anecdote illustrates the fall from an industrial society towards a service society, where the largely unskilled proletariat is found among supermarket cashiers, nursing assistants in retirement homes, and Uber Eats delivery persons. Today, France has less than 10 per cent of the labour force counted in the industrial sector, a figure that we also see in the United States and in the United Kingdom. De-industrialization has emptied whole territories of their lifeblood. Industry adapts to distant territories where the cost of real estate is low: it's the merchandise that travels. Tertiarization has produced an entirely new geography. Jobs are at the heart of metropolises, closest to the customer. Workers, after being driven out of the factories, have been expelled from the cities, where the price of housing is too high, and they have to cope with longer commutes and transportation costs that are constantly rising.

In addition to jobs themselves, it is the whole sociology of the working classes that has been affected. The geographer Arnaud Frémont grasped it in the triptych: 'factory – housing project – stadium'. De-industrialization has destroyed the dense life of the workers, in the factory and outside it, of which the Communist Party was the political expression. Worker's housing estates were sold off piecemeal or destroyed. Municipalities have sometimes taken them back to develop them as social housing, occupied by groups that are socially fragile, precarious or unemployed. Football clubs also played an essential role in workers' culture, and were often supported by large industrial groups. The Greens of Saint-Étienne were one of the memorable examples of this. Today, 'sponsoring' continues, but it is no longer in the service of the local population. The FC Sochaux, supported by the Peugeot family since 1928, had created a very strong bond between the car maker and the workers. The club was later sold, the firm preferring to sponsor tennis, a sport 'that is more in agreement with our values – that is, international, and that interests women as much as it does men' (and that the Peugeot group finally abandoned as well). De-industrialization has provoked a shock that quickly became irreversible in the regions most affected. When the most mobile inhabitants, the most qualified ones, leave industrial zones, the latter rapidly lose the critical mass making it possible to attract sophisticated services, especially in the domain of health or education. The vice of social solitude closes on those who remain.

A Political Revolution

This feeling of isolation, of social distress, was to have immense consequences, of which the election of Donald Trump in 2016 was to mark the climax on the political terrain. His victory took observers by surprise, as much as did Brexit, the election of Salvini in Italy, and that of Bolsonaro in Brazil.

With this election, the polarization of American political life reached a summit, bringing to incandescence the war being waged between two Americas who have lost all respect for each other. To the question 'Would you be unhappy if your child married a Democrat?', 5 per cent of Republicans answered in the affirmative in 1960, and now 50 per cent of them do. The same detestation is seen in the case of questions bearing on the intelligence or honesty of the adverse camp.[14] Political polarization is also found in the geography of the votes. Counties that voted Republican or Democrat did so much more clearly than they did thirty years ago. Biden's voters and Trump's do not live in the same America. Democrats live for the most part in big cities, and those who live in small ones or rural zones voted for Trump. Several studies have shown that Trump's election was closely correlated with the flare-up of social solitude in the lower classes of which Case and Deaton painted such a desperate picture.[15] The clearest sign that the questions of social disconnection have become central can be gauged by the crushing eruption of identity issues in political debate. Politics used to speak a language of social classes, workers, bourgeois, and redistribution. Today, people talk about 'identities', whether these are racial or national.

In his book *What's the matter with Kansas?*, Thomas Frank painted a disillusioned portrait of the former industrial city of Wichita, Kansas, which had been to aeronautics what Detroit was to the automobile. With the closure of the factories that gave it its working-class identity, it became the capital of the new Right, apparently haunted by the single obsession of becoming the vanguard of opposition to abortion. This hiatus between the de-industrialization that patently raises the social question, on the one hand, and the political reaction that moved onto the cultural terrain, on the other hand, is a mystery that each commentator tries to resolve in his/her own way. For authors like Inglehart and Norris, the cultural question is a backlash on the part of those who have still not digested the cultural revolution of the 1960s, and who express it in their vote for the Right.[16] What doesn't work in this explanation is that voting for the far Right is not in any way limited to elderly people, as Norris and Inglehart suggest. Young people are no less numerous in supporting the extreme Right. Seeing in the movement towards the hard Right merely the last embers of a generation overtaken by the cultural practices of later generations just doesn't make sense.

Another explanation is that the class war that used to bear on questions of redistribution is now being fought on the terrain of immigration. The latter is taken to be an objective fact, a major one, which has de-structured working-class identities and which left-wing parties, by virtue of their internationalist leaning, have not succeeded in admitting.[17] This explanation has at least the merit of sticking more closely to the discourse of those concerned, who make xenophobia their main warhorse. All the parties that embody this new populism on the Right in fact share a strong xenophobic tint, even in the Scandinavian countries, which were, nonetheless, better protected from the crisis and the rise of inequalities. The Sweden Democrats, the Danish People's Party, the True Finns Party, the Freedom Party of Austria, the Golden Dawn party in Greece, the League in Italy, are all constructed on a xenophobic discourse. The French Front National, which has now been renamed the National Rally, is completely emblematic of this movement.

However, that is not the only thing that unites them. For example, xenophobia is perfectly correlated with homophobia. For Tabellini and his co-authors, this has to do with a cumulative phenomenon. Once the issue of identity has been raised, it draws nourishment from considerations other than the ones that gave it birth. But in that case it becomes possible to invert the argument and say that the theme of immigration can itself be the effect of another cause. In his book *L'Archipel français*, Jérôme Fourquet has analysed the correlation between voting for the extreme Right leader Marine Le Pen and the presence of a Muslim community, by spotting the first names of children in each of the communes. Votes for Le Pen are fewer in communes where Muslim first names are rare, rise in proportion to the increase in the latter, and attain a high point when these first names constitute more than a third of births. This reversal is itself easy to interpret: when Muslims are numerous, the racists leave. However, the most interesting point is to consider the communes where there is literally no child bearing a Muslim first name. Their vote for the extreme Right is, to be sure, smaller than average, but not by all that much. It won almost 17 per cent of the votes, compared with a national score of 23 per cent. This is a sign that something besides xenophobia and racism is expressed in the shift of politics towards questions of identity.

The answer we give in our book *Les Origines du populisme* is close to Durkheim's explanation of suicide.[18] Social anomie and the aversion to the rest of society that itself results from the rarefaction of social ties create an identitarian impulse that wins out over the classic questions of social classes and redistribution. Under an apparent continuity with the traditional Right's electorate, Le Pen's partisans are profoundly wary, not only with regard to institutions, but also with regard to other people. To the question, 'Can you trust a stranger met by chance, or do you think you can never be too cautious?' they are pathologically numerous in choosing distrust. The latter's range is extensive: it applies not only to strangers but also to colleagues and neighbours. The far Right's distrust is much more acute than that of the classic Right. The latter is traditionalist, proprietary: it distrusts the dangerous classes. Le Pen voters' distrust is deeper; it reflects their difficulty in making a society in a world that is constantly fragmenting individual destinies more and more.

Hatred of democracy

The new violence of each political camp with regard to others is also the mark of a profound decline of the democratic ideal.[19] To the question, 'Is democracy the best system or could another system be just as good as democracy?', more than one French person thinks that another system might be just as good.[20] Voters' judgement of their representatives is cruel: for 87% of European citizens and 88% of American citizens, 'most political officials defend their own interests first of all, and are not concerned with people like me'. In terms of the rate of confidence, hospitals and small and medium-sized businesses are at 75%, parliament at 35%, and political parties at 15%! Political officials are thought to be corrupt by 77% of European citizens – with a record of 91% in Hungary and Poland – and by 79% of Americans. The radicalization of political life is also encountered in a growing abstention and in an unprecedented vote for the most radical parties.

This political distrust can also be seen in the parties' loss of influence. During the French presidential election in 2022, they all almost disappeared from the voters' radar. Macron, Le Pen, Mélenchon, and Zemmour, the four leading candidates, have in common that they created a party in their own image (except for Le Pen, who inherited one from her father). This transmutation expresses the encounter between a public opinion that no longer supports the constituted bodies and a Fifth Republic in which everything is summed up in the election of a man or a woman. This tendency towards the de-institutionalization of political life is present in a very great number of countries. One of the 'structuring' elements of populist parties such as the Five Star Movement or the League in Italy, is that they construct anti-party parties. A detailed study by Cas Mudde distinguishes two gradations in this attitude.[21] The first is the critique of governing parties on the basis of the failure of the policies they have pursued. That is what happened when, in Greece for example, the Socialist Party was replaced by a party further to the left, Syriza, which nonetheless ended up becoming a governing party in its turn.

A more radical critique challenges the very idea of parties. Political officials are considered corrupt, more attached to pursuing their careers than to the welfare of their fellow citizens. The solution, according to this argument, is to create movements guided by a charismatic leader who dissolves the opposition between the masses and the elites by a fusion between the leader and the people in a way redolent of the 1930s. As Mudde emphasizes, the difference nonetheless has to do with the fact that at the time democracy was still a new idea, in Italy or in Germany in particular: the detestation of parties went hand in hand with a more general detestation of a still-young democracy. Today, the discourses against parties proceed from inside democracy. Parties, which are supposed to keep democracy alive, are no longer considered democratic.

Michel Offerlé, in the conclusion of his book on political parties, ironically echoes this accusation: 'Vertical apparatuses are in crisis: the voter wants the truth to be told, he no longer makes decisions on the basis of great ideologies but rather on the stakes and the images [...] The crisis in militancy also testifies to this. The return to individualism implies less all-encompassing commitments. [...] Reading this summary', Offerlé adds, 'one senses what's blowing in the air.' But political parties 'take a long time to die'. Their role is not so easy to replace. When a worker voted for the Communist Party, he/she was adhering to its central values, the collective ownership of the means of production, but also the equality of men and women, as well as internationalism, which put their internal world in sync with the world at large.

The crisis of parties adds political anomie to social anomie.

Vox populi

The birth of the internet galaxy bore the promise of a new democratic regime, a veritable planetary agora. Worldwide movements such as Me Too, Black Lives Matter, and Extinction Rebellion, are part of this new international community, whose most glorious feats of arms are to have made insurrections against dictatorships possible. The Arab Spring in 2010 or the revolution in Ukraine in 2014 emerged from their guts. New social movements, from Occupy Wall Street to the Yellow Vests in France, also provide examples.

However, social networks are not succeeding in producing a genuine deliberative space. 'Instead of supporting living together, [they] support the fractures, cleavages, and crumbling from which contemporary society suffers.'[22] Democracy is simultaneously a mode of government and an art of living together. Social networks are devoured by an economy that demands the spectacular and the detestation of one's rivals. As Edgar Morin puts it, 'For the past two decades, we have been witnessing, in the world and also in France, the growth of Manicheanism, unilateral visions, hatreds and scorn.' The digital revolution is obviously not the direct cause of this tension that is spreading in society, but it provides an unprecedented sounding board for it. Samuel Paty, a French teacher who was beheaded by an Islamist radical, was denounced on social networks as an enemy of Islam, and it sufficed that an assassin took it into his head to kill him.

There are, to be sure, ideologues who maintain tensions, but for the philosopher Cyrille Bret, interviewed by *Le Monde*, the savagery of contemporary social life is due in large part to this online violence, where anyone who expresses a contrary opinion is an enemy and can be threatened. In Freudian terms, we could say that social networks dissociate the Superego and the Id, without the mediation of the Ego. There are networks of Superegos, Facebook and Instagram, where people display themselves as being as beautiful as possible, where smiling selfies are multiplied, and where everything is photographed, including food. And there is the Id, the seat of desires, left to itself, masked by anonymity, liberating the hatreds and cruelties that lie dormant in society.

Even in groups as innocent as that of amateur tennis players, one can't help being struck by the violence that is expressed here, Nadal's fans manifesting an obscene hatred for the admirers of Federer or Djokovic. A mild-mannered American site specializing in popular science had to close its comments pages, having been submerged by the attacks of creationists who found its articles intolerable. One anecdote sums up the power of the nauseating culture that circulates on the Net. One of Microsoft's programs, educating itself on American social networks in an 'unsupervised' way, quickly became racist, 'white supremacist', by absorbing the culture diffused on the sites it had visited. It is on such sites (and in prisons), far more than in mosques, that Islamists are recruited. In each case, the goal is to take revenge on a society that ignores you, to do whatever it takes to attract attention to yourself, including filming your own death, once you have murdered someone else.

Obviously, it would be absurd to impute the rise of populism to Facebook accounts alone. The 1930s did not wait for them. Nonetheless, their role is real. Thus, an experiment was able to establish the direct responsibility of social networks in this culture of hatred. A study bearing on 3,000 people analysed the effects of deactivating their Facebook accounts for a month.[23] At the end of this diet, the extremist penchants of the subscribers had decreased considerably. Better yet, when they were authorized to resume contact with the network, their consumption of social media decreased, as if they had been cured of their addictive behaviours. After the experiment, 80 per cent of the people involved recognized that the deactivation had done them good.

The wisdom of crowds

Trump's election became famous for the introduction of 'fake news' into political debate. Sites that were notorious for propagating false reports (on which less than 50 per cent of the information listed is 'serious') supported Trump in a totally disproportionate way. In the month preceding the election, about a hundred cases of fake news in his favour were shared more than 30 million times on the social networks, compared with only forty favourable to Hillary Clinton, which were shared only 7.6 million times.[24] How can we understand this unexpected paradox from a technology designed to make it possible to converse with others, to exchange ideas – in short, to nourish democratic debate – which ended up establishing an almost exactly opposite system: 'fake news', characterized by violence and hatred?

Kahneman and his co-authors offer an initial way of understanding this paradox, by returning to an article entitled 'Vox populi', published in 1907 by Francis Galton. Galton himself was a sulphurous figure. A nephew of Darwin, he had rapidly made himself the propagandist for 'social Darwinism', a theory according to which the work of natural selection had to be continued by human beings themselves, an idea that is at the foundation of eugenics and Nazism. Whatever his terrible penchants might have been, Galton had published an article that was later to give rise to numerous verifications, making it possible to measure what James Suroweicki, the author who rediscovered Galton's article, was to call 'the wisdom of crowds'.

Galton had asked a group of 787 villagers to guess the weight of a piece of beef that had been hung up in a public square. None of them was able to guess the correct weight, but – and this is extraordinary – the average of the answers turned out to be very close (it was 1 kilo off). Identical results were obtained in slew of contexts. Crowds were asked to guess the number of beans contained in a transparent bowl, the number of crimes committed in a city, the length of a border between two countries. Each time, the average of the responses was extremely precise. For statisticians, this was a possible application of the law of large numbers: the average of a sample tends, under certain hypotheses, to converge on the correct figure. Two authors pushed the experiment a little further: they asked one person to give a second opinion after having made his first estimate. The average of the two estimates was more accurate than either of them. The authors of the study called this 'the crowd within'.[25]

To understand what happens with social networks, we have to analyse what happens when the different people assembled for a survey are authorized to talk with one another. As soon as information on the estimates proposed by others is made available to them (for example, those of a dozen or so people chosen at random), the aggregated results become extremely bad. The crowds that were wise fall into the trap of what is called 'informational cascades', in which the ideas of a few people find an echo that is much too large, considerably reducing the quality of the average judgement. If I learn that my neighbour has made a certain estimate of the piece of beef's weight, I will hesitate to make my own estimate, and I will come round to the one I think is better informed. Listening to me, my own neighbours will come round to my opinion.

Ultimately, it is the opinion of a single person that will win out, even though it is only one view among others, no matter what his competences may be. His opinion will silence, from the height of his supposed expertise, the multitude of points of view whose errors would be compensated in the average if they had been allowed to express themselves freely. As A. Banerjee has demonstrated in a fundamental article entitled 'Herd behaviour', it is not irrational for an isolated individual to rally to an opinion that he considers to be of better quality. But if the process leads, de facto, to a silencing of timid opinions, the result will be an immense informational loss for the collectivity.

Kahneman and his co-authors propose a very large number of real situations that confirm this result. Analysing the results of a jury's deliberations, they show how the latter often tend to yield judgments that are much more radical than foreseen. The most eloquent of the jury's members becomes ascendant over the others and stifles the noise of small differences, from which, however, a balanced judgment might arise.[26] When the members of a group listen to each other, the undecided ones will rally to what they will interpret as the dominant opinion, and their 'moderating' virtues will be muffled. It is not necessary to go further to understand how social networks end up betraying their original promise.

Beliefs and information

Another factor has contributed to the degradation of public debate: the declining number of journalists. In the United States, there are only half as many as there were in the 1980s. It follows that there is a considerable loss in the quality of the information provided. In permanent competition with social media, the profession has gradually changed in nature. In the new digital world, 'news' soon becomes obsolete, displaced by other, more promising 'news'. This programmed obsolescence is radically changing journalistic practice. The quest for 'scoops' that attract attention and provoke in their turn informational cascades in their favour becomes more interesting than the costly quest for information that risks being lost in the flux of actuality. Instead of producing, for example, a detailed analysis of the budget presented to the National Assembly, a journalist will be much more interested in finding the salient fact that will allow him to denounce the budget exercise in its totality and to attract attention to his own analysis.

As Julia Cagé showed in her thesis, the rise in the number of media paradoxically leads to an impoverishment of the quality of the information received by each of their readers.[27] Under the impact of increasingly tough competition, each kind of media is impoverished. Even if the mass of information is increased on the whole, the one that users consume individually becomes smaller. Studying the French regional dailies, Cagé showed that the appearance of a new medium in a geographic pool led ultimately to an increase in political abstention! Her conclusion was clear and iconoclastic. It's not the media that must be supported – doing so can only help to increase competitive pressure; instead, we have to support the quality of information, by lending support upstream, to the news agencies.

But the fundamental point is that social networks are in reality not at all interested in information in the ordinary sense of the term. What they produce online are beliefs that flatter the sensitivities of their members. The distinction between information and beliefs is a crucial point that has been stressed by Roland Bénabou and Jean Tirole in their works.[28] Their approach is different from the analysis in which each individual relies on the opinion of others, for lack of certainties. Many of the examples they study show that people really believe in the ideas they profess, even in extreme cases where prudence should be appropriate. Thus, during the subprime crisis, many investors bought their own houses at the top of the bubble, which proves that they really believed in the durability of the boom.

Beliefs do not help us interpret the world, they help us live in it. I am happy to believe in Santa Claus, it's a comforting idea, and it saddens me to learn that he does not exist. I'll reject the bad news as long as I can.[29] People treat good and bad news in totally asymmetrical ways: they reject the bad news and concentrate on the good. Thus, it has been shown that non-professional investors check the value of their own portfolios when the stock market is bullish and don't check it when it turns bearish. They seek to escape the news that bothers them. This is a mechanism very different from the sheep-like effects in which each individual copies another, for lack of pertinent information; here, people deliberately obliterate information that would ruin their life. When a panel of people is asked where they think they are situated in this or that domain (humour or beauty), the great majority will answer that they are in the first or second quarter. No one will situate himself in the last two quarters, even though, by definition, half of the population should be found there.[30] Everyone wants to keep his self-confidence, think he's desirable, admired for his good looks, his intelligence, or his sense of humour!

Playing lotto and buying insurance policies

In a world of pure rationality, beliefs should be refutable. I believe that the weather will be fine; I consult the weather report, I learn that it will be cold, and I put on an overcoat. I learn that the planet is warming; I deduce from this that I have to act. Things don't happen that way. If I'm a Republican and I read a study showing that global warming is a mortal danger, I don't change my opinion. I challenge the scope of the study, convince myself that it's not scientific, that it was financed by Green parties whose opinion is biased. A Republican who acknowledges that the planet is warming becomes a renegade, obliged to political exile.[31] If we think about the mortal controversies that accompanied the Copernican Revolution, it is clear what is at stake. Admitting that the Earth turns around the Sun is accompanied by a radical challenge to a whole system of thought. It is the relation to the Scriptures, to revealed truths, that is shaken.

If, to return to the conclusions of an American study, an opinion appears to have Democratic sensitivities because a medium reputed to be left-wing supported it, the idea in question will spread to other Democrats and will generate an instinctive hostility among Republicans. The same obviously holds when the opinion is supposed to emanate from Republicans. As the researchers who conducted this analysis conclude, opinions that are a priori centrist can rapidly become the stake in bloody battles between opposing camps.

Marcel Proust summed up the problem magnificently:

> The facts of life do not penetrate to the sphere in which our beliefs are cherished; they did not engender those beliefs, and they are powerless to destroy them; they can inflict on them continual blows of contradiction and disproof without

weakening them; and an avalanche of miseries and maladies succeeding one another without interruption in the bosom of a family will not make it lose faith in either the clemency of its God or the capacity of its physician.

Beliefs have an entirely different function than to enlighten us regarding the world, they are a treasure that helps us to live, internally and with others. We choose our beliefs the way a consumer chooses in a big department store, depending on fashions and what is for sale on the shelves.

Our beliefs are, in the language of Robert Abelson, an asset that we would like to turn to good account and that has to be protected against adverse winds. The economist George Loewenstein gives a very interesting example that illustrates this property. Imagine that you are offered a choice between a cake today and another in a month. You will almost certainly choose the cake today, present consumption always being more desirable than future consumption. Symmetrically, if you have to pay a fine of 10 euros today and you are invited to pay it in a month, you will certainly choose to delay the payment. Now imagine that you are given the following choice: either to be electro-shocked today, or to delay it for a month. Everything, in the economic argument, should lead you to put it off. But often it is the contrary that happens.[32] Most people prefer to suffer it today, to have it over with! Because you don't want the shock to spoil your imagination.

Other economic paradoxes are illuminated by this perspective. Why do people buy lottery tickets and insurance policies at the same time? To insure oneself is to have fear of risk, playing lotto is the opposite: it's to love it. The answer that economists have always struggled to give is immediate in the framework renewed by Loewenstein: I want to dream of the radiant future promised by the lottery ticket, and at the same time feel protected against the accidents of life, which is procured by insurance. Even if it seems totally contradictory to the canons of economic analysis, the life of the mind does in fact have at its disposal rigorous rules that all aim at the same result: to make us dream, and drive away sad thoughts.

Beliefs regarding oneself or the world are not 'objective' information, but rather a good that you cherish, that gives you joy and that you want to protect against bad news (Santa Claus doesn't exist, sorry!). Reality isn't the good we seek to reach; on the contrary, it's the obstacle to the satisfaction provided by dreams. The digital supply puts at our disposal an almost infinite ability to find ideas that suit us. You think 11 September was a trick set up by the CIA? On the Net, you'll find a million people who think as you do. Their thinking will support yours. The Net fabricates a world in accord with our desires.

That is more or less the promise of hard drugs, the remedy and cause for contemporary despair.

Part II

The Return of Reality

5

Social Ties

The Law of 150 Friends

At first, the Internet was seen as the promise of a new collective intelligence, the platform of a reinvented democracy. Instead, social networks have given rise to a tremendous dumbing down of political life and to a growth of the disease that they were supposed to cure: social solitude. How was such a disillusionment possible? In large measure, the answer to that question has to do with a misunderstanding due to the free-market illusion. For the latter, a society can institute itself by aggregating isolated individuals, without mediation, without rites of passage, without intermediary bodies, provided that they are given means of 'communicating' with each other. But the whole history of societies is, on the contrary, moulded by the life of institutions, churches or parties, sects or enterprises, that permeate the consciousnesses of individuals and offer them the means to rise above the few networks that their interactions are likely to produce.

To grasp the role of these institutions, an excellent point of departure is provided by the anthropologist Robin Dunbar, the author who introduced us, through Shakespeare, to the levels of human intentionality. The latter enable us to understand the immense difficulty of conceiving the utopia of a society in which every individual could potentially enter into dialogue with others. Dunbar begins from an explosive statistical observation: there is, he says, a significant correlation between the density of the social relations of the different species and the size of their brains! Primates such as baboons, macaques, and chimpanzees live in sophisticated social environments and also have the largest neocortexes. For not only does the brain allow us to think, it is the central factor allowing us to live in society. The Darwinian line of reasoning no doubt leads us to explain this correlation: species whose survival depends on collective action have ended up being caused by natural selection to have larger brains.

For Dunbar, intentionality also increases with the size of the brain. According to his calculations, 2 million years ago *Homo erectus* had arrived at third-order intentionality, in view of the estimated size of their brains. They were the first to be able to conceive the sentence: 'I know that you think that I'm thinking about you.' It is possible that fourth-order intentionality was reached 500,000 years ago, among archaic humans. The last stage was attained about 300,000 years ago, when modern humans appeared, reaching fifth-order intentionality. This was the time when the human species developed culture and religion.

If we extrapolate the connection between the volume of the brain and the density of primates' social life, what size of human communities can be predicted? The number obtained is known as the 'Dunbar law': the maximal number of people with whom one can maintain social relationships is 150! An impressive list of social structures obeys this rule. Thus, the Roman army's basic unit, the maniple, consisted of about 150 soldiers;[1] the size of English villages, as estimated by William the Conqueror's scribes in a census known as

Domesday, in 1086, included a number surprisingly close to 150. The same holds for English villages in the eighteenth century. The Hutterites and the Amish, two North American religious groups (the former live in Western Canada and the northern Great Plains of the United States; the latter live in Pennsylvania and were popularized by the film *Witness*, starring Harrison Ford) split their communities into two as soon as they pass the threshold of 150 members. In an entirely different domain, Dunbar and his colleague Russell Hill conducted an investigation of the number of Christmas cards sent. Similarly, they found an average of 150! In the world of business, the founder of Gore-Tex has always insisted that the units of production in his company should not exceed this optimal size of 150 people. Estimates of the same kind have been made in scientific communities. The number of researchers whose works an individual is capable of following is also located between 100 and 200.

Today, does Facebook do much better than that? A survey by the Pew Research Center has shown that Facebook users have, on average, 338 'friends'. Does Facebook double the capacities of our brains? That seems unlikely; if, disregarding friends who are merely named, we limit ourselves to the sub-set of those with whom real communication is established, we will probably arrive at a number not far from the maximum of 150. Obviously, that does not prevent the Web, as its name indicates, from connecting an anthill of interlinked networks: 150 multiplied by 150 several times would rapidly cover the whole of the Earth's surface.

An old inquiry conducted by Stanley Milgram in the mid-1960s showed what he called a 'degree of separation', which measured the number of intermediaries necessary to transmit a unit of information from an individual A to an individual B who was unknown to the former. Milgram asked farmers in Kansas to send a letter to a person living in Massachusetts who was a priori completely unknown to them. In one of the examples, the farmer, A, had sent the letter to his pastor, who sent it to his colleague in Cambridge, who knew individual B directly. The experiment showed that, in general, the number of contacts necessary was close to six. The same experiment was carried out on Facebook. The average number of contacts between two users without a priori links between them was close to four.[2] Thus Facebook allows us to gain two stages in the process of connecting the world. That is certainly useful, but it does not suffice, in itself, to shape a new society! The whole history of civilizations consists in developing systems of relationship and interdependence, in drawing on culture or religion to bring humans together far beyond the mere play of their interactions, no matter how optimized they may be.

That's what the digital revolution has lacked up to now.

Bonobos and Chimpanzees

La Fontaine could have written a fable about 'The chimpanzee and the bonobo' to shed light on the possibilities of the social world explored by our simian cousins. Bonobos make love; chimpanzees wage war. The bonobo is emotional, sensitive. His long-winded sexuality is a calming factor. Chimpanzees are more aggressive; their social relations are tenser. How can we explain such a difference? The biologist Alain Prochiantz notes that these two species are almost identical on the level of their genomes: they differ by only 0.4 per cent. Why are their social characteristics so different? According to the anthropologist Evan MacLean, quoted by Prochiantz, the economy plays a major role. The two species developed on opposite sides of the Congo River. Chimpanzees were on the bad side, where food was scarce, while bonobos benefitted from a more favourable environment. According to MacLean, the relative abundance of food explains the bonobos' more cooperative, more social attitude. Conversely, the chimpanzee is not inclined to cooperate. One who discovers food almost never shares it with his fellows. Female chimpanzees are much more individualist; they do not make alliances among themselves.[3]

If the fable of the bonobo and the chimpanzee contains something that might interest us, it would be that it says that abundance makes cooperation more 'natural' and shortage of food makes society more 'competitive'. The fact that the 'hippie' movements or those of May 1968 appeared at the heart of a society of abundance confirms the prevalence in this case of the bonobo slogan: 'Make love, not war.' That the conservative revolution won a foothold during lean years is also logical according to this line of reasoning. What doesn't work in this theory, obviously, is that advanced societies were no poorer in the 1980s than they were in the 1960s. That does not necessarily make the fable false, but it does require that its concept be clarified. Among humans, everything (or almost) is relative, at least in societies that have raised themselves above a certain threshold of subsistence. We aren't richer or poorer in the absolute sense, but relative to other people, or relative to our expectations. Thus we are obliged to conclude that it is their own conditions of social existence that make humans lean towards one or another of their potentialities, the bonobo type or the chimpanzee type.

Confidence and reciprocity

The chimpanzee/bonobo debate is of great interest to economists, because it presents the data for a question on which their own discipline depends: are humans spontaneously 'cooperative', society making them 'competitive', or are they, as Hobbes thought, wolves for humans (*homo homini lupus est*) that society makes more peaceful? For Mancur Olson (to whom we owe the concept of a 'free rider'), as soon as the size of a group becomes too large and relations with others become anonymous, humans lose the glue of affection that connects them to one another and egoism becomes the rule. However, Elinor Ostrom, who received the Nobel Prize for Economics for her works on public goods, shows that there exist many situations in which the public space is respected by the communities concerned, with no motive other than the spontaneous adhesion of its members to the public good. It is not always necessary to set fines or prison sentences to make citizens obey laws. A text by Nicolas Jacquemet and his co-authors shows that, despite cases of fraud, taxpayers pay their taxes in a way that cannot be rationalized by economic calculus alone.[4] Taxpayers, at least the great majority of them, behave in a way that only 'morality' and the spirit of civic responsibility can explain.

In fact, there are many experimental proofs that demonstrate that care for others is 'innate', like language itself, and not just a cog in a sophisticated calculation for obtaining a deferred reward by being nice to someone.[5] Leon Festinger, to whom we owe the concept of cognitive dissonance, says that an individual cannot create a concept of himself in the absence of a group identity. To betray one's group is to betray oneself. A game called 'The Ultimatum' shows that a logic of honour haunts our relation to others and defines us ourselves. In this game, two people who do not know each other and will never see each other again agree to divide 10 dollars between them. The first (call him A) decides to allocate x to himself and $10-x$ to the other (call him B), but it is the second who has to say whether he accepts this division or not. If he refuses it, the 10 dollars will be burned; if he accepts it, the division is made.

If B is obsessed with a strictly opportunistic and rational economic calculation, he should accept the share offered by person A, no matter what it is. For B, in fact, the choice is 'something or nothing'. Even if A offers him only 1 dollar, keeping the 9 others for himself, that should still be something to take. The game shows that this is clearly not at all the case. B cannot accept the humiliation of an excessively unfavourable divvying-up. His choices are guided more by anger and indignation than by rational calculation. Moreover, experience allows us to show, inversely, the influence of good humour on the conduct of this negotiation. If a comic video is shown to the two participants and they laugh together at the same gags, participant A becomes as generous with B as he would be with a life-long friend. Laughter, and especially collective laughter, has the particularity of transforming strangers into friends.

A key concept that also emerges from this type of experiment is the notion of reciprocity. Another 'laboratory' experiment, the 'Trust Game', illustrates what it involves. Two people, each in front of a computer screen, are confronted with the following situation. At the beginning of the experiment, the first player, the 'sender', Mr S, is offered 50 dollars. He can leave with that sum, and in that case the experiment is over. But he can also send all or part of the sum to the other player, the 'receiver', Mr. R. In this case, he multiplies by three the sum sent. Mr. R can in turn leave with the tripled sum which was sent to him, and then the game is interrupted. But he can also, without receiving any counterpart, send all or part of his profit to Mr. S, and then the game is really over.

Confronted by this game, a 'rational' economic agent should reason this way: if I send 'my' dollars to the other player, he will certainly receive a tripled sum, but what interest would he then have in sending them back to me? None: he doesn't know me, and will never see me again. Knowing that, I send nothing. What is the result of the experiment? It is once again the opposite. A large majority of the participants send part of the sum they are allocated, and in two-thirds of the cases they are rewarded. Why, then, send the money if it is perfectly useless from an egoistic point of view? The traditional economic line of argument has no reply.[6] Psychologists and philosophers speak of reciprocity, a concept half-way between altruism and individualism.[7] It designates the desire to respond to generosity with generosity, without any reward other than that of being worthy of the trust that has been accorded to you.[8]

The Trust Game, like The Ultimatum, also allows us to test the influence of good humour on cooperation. When the operator receives a dose of oxytocin, a drug that puts people in a good humour, reciprocity increases. 'Happiness' does in fact make humans more disposed to share! But good humour also has surprising effects: it can anaesthetize our critical spirit. Gordon Pennycook and his colleagues have studied people's reaction to meaningless statements.[9] Pseudo-profound statements such as 'The whole calms infinite phenomena' or 'The hidden meaning transforms unequalled abstract beauty' are presented to the subjects of the study. The propensity to be in agreement with such statements is a trait known under the name of 'receptivity to bullshit'.[10] Good humour augments it. Another surprising consequence of good humour is to modify the moral sense. In the tramway example, the subjects put in a positive mood by seeing a video 5 minutes long became 3 times more likely to push their neighbour onto the tracks in order to avoid the death of the 5 passengers.

In the company of strangers

In his book *The Company of Strangers*, Paul Seabright highlights humans' astonishing propensity to trust people unknown to them.[11] Other species, he stresses, collaborate with their fellows without family relationships – 'stickle-backs, bats, lions' – but only occasionally. Some species obviously need one another, as do sharks and their pilot-fish, but that is a matter of ecological complementarities between species that do not communicate with each other.

The propensity to reciprocity with strangers is the foundation of the social world. But it is only a necessary condition, not a sufficient one. Without suitable institutions, it can just as well lead to perpetual vendetta as to saintliness. Reciprocity leads to one sequence – 'You give, I return' – or to another: 'You betray me, I take revenge.' Once the spiral of suspicion is launched, how can we prevent it from degenerating? Even within married couples, it is sometimes difficult to interrupt a quarrel. In a very funny book,[12] Paul Watzlawick shows how a couple can fall into the abyss if they do not have ways of saying, 'I don't like your porridge but I do love you.' We have to have a metalanguage, a language about language, in order to really understand one another. Watzlawick suggests, for instance, saying 'The porridge has an amusing taste', to suggest to one's spouse that you're really talking about breakfast and not the love relationship.

On the scale of society *in toto*, there are whole regions in Sicily or Albania that have been decimated by the eternal cycle of the vendetta.[13] To stop it, people need supra-individual institutions to which a 'monopoly on legitimate violence' is entrusted, to adopt Max Weber's formula. The ability to produce a social order through the reciprocity of the participants is just as fantastic as the inverse idea that society could endure through coercion alone. Nor does the logic of self-interest suffice to make a society. If you were facing someone without any sense of honour, just opportunistic in his desire to make a profit, how could you simply do business with him without fearing that he is seeking to cheat you? When you're on a plane, you don't want to rely on the airline's interest to ensure that you are safe. You want to think that there is a professional group, that of pilots, which has its traditions, and that a logic of honour guarantees the moral integrity of its members. Criminals themselves have their codes, even if that will not suffice for us to entrust the management of the world to them.

'Belonging' to an institution

An institution, whether an airline company or a mafia, is far more than the 'contract node' that economists like to describe, a view according to which each individual acts in order to achieve an immediate or deferred gratification. Herbert Simon, one of the great scientists who were to contribute to the development of AI and who received the Nobel Prize for Economics in 1978, has strongly criticized this idea. An enterprise, he explains, is a place that gives a meaning to the lives of its members, and not one where the suffering they undergo is rewarded with a salary.[14]

In the introduction to the collective volume *Sociologie de l'institution*, Jacques Lagroye and Michel Offerlé stressed the immense variety of the ways in which an individual 'belongs to an institution'. Whether it is a way of belonging to a company, a labour union or a political party, it is always a matter of adhering to a mode of thought. For Mary Douglas, the institution provides its members with 'mental categories, establishes their self-consciousness, and stabilizes their identity'. Bourdieu also underlines the power of rites of passage: 'investiture exercises a symbolic efficacy that is entirely real, insofar as it really transforms the person'. Foucault goes still further. He attributes to the institution's 'disciplinary power' the ability to standardize human beings, to inculcate in them a specific identity, and to exercise on them 'the constraint of a conformity to be exercised'.

Erving Goffman's works nonetheless warn us against an excessively rigid interpretation of the role of institutions. Even in the extreme cases represented by asylums, 'the individual is a being capable of distanciation, that is, capable of adopting a position intermediate between identification with institutions and opposition to them'. For Goffman, an agent who limits himself to embracing the goals of the institution 'with too much enthusiasm' may in fact prove to be embarrassing, even lethal, for the latter. Overly zealous police officers, persnickety bureaucrats, and excessively strict grammar school monitors do not help the institution they believe they are defending. Goffman's point of view emphasizes the subtlety of the relation that is established between the institution and the person who adheres to it.

As Albert Hirschman has also made clear, members of an institution have at their disposition several possible ways of participating in the life of the group. Hirschman sums them up in a trilogy: 'Exit, voice, and loyalty'. Exit: it is possible to leave the institution. Voice: members can try to renovate it (by speaking up). Loyalty: members obey its rules without discussion. In the work edited by Lagroye and Offerlé, Yann Raison du Cleuziou analyses very subtly the way May 1968 disrupted the Dominican order by making demands in these three registers at once. Permeated by the events of May, some young people demanded reforms suited to the new times (voice), while older ones, obsessed with respect for the order of things, were against any response to these demands (loyalty), and others, finally, chose to leave (exit) for other orders, or simply to live outside the religious institution.

The works of Roland Bénabou illustrate perfectly the way in which tension between the collective credo and individual calculation can be established at the heart of certain social groups.[15] In the numerous examples that he analyses, the possibility of leaving the group – Exit – plays a key role. In traditional communities in which no exit is possible, loyalty is the only way to live serenely. Similarly, if you're a sailor on the *Titanic*, you're better off thinking that the captain knows what he's doing: doubting it wouldn't advance the cause and it would prevent you from properly carrying out your mission. We can also add that a high cost of entry explains the loyalty

to an institution. If you have expended a great deal of effort
to belong to it, whether it be the US Marines or the high ranks
of the civil service, it is certain that you wanted to adhere to
its values, even beyond what your own values were before
you entered the group. Otherwise, you would feel that you'd
spoiled the best years of your life for nothing.[16] But if there
is an easy way to leave the institution – whether it consists,
for example, of a couple or an enterprise – you will be more
inclined to express yourself (Voice) or leave it (Exit).[17]

No matter how these threads of belonging are knotted
together, analysing human civilizations requires grasping all
the subtlety of the logics in which moral affects, religious or
secular convictions, and the mechanisms of sanctions that
regulate the social world are mixed. As summed up perfectly
by Paul Seabright, the fundamental point of institutions is to
'allow a small number of regulations to go a long way in the
organization of society'.

Where is the digital revolution taking us?

Four Possible Societies

To situate the digital world on the grand scale of human
history, we have to return to the different ways in which
societies have succeeded in bringing humans together. Let
us distinguish two possible axes. From the point of view of
individual interactions, first of all, societies can be of a vertical
or a horizontal type, depending on whether they are organized
according to hierarchical or egalitarian principles. Next, from
the point of view of their collective psyche, societies can be
religious or secular, depending on whether they believe in
divine or scientific laws. This yields four possible combinations: egalitarian/religious, hierarchical/religious, hierarchical/
secular, and horizontal/secular. It is this last type to which
digital society is giving birth. Let us make a tour of the ways
in which other types have been deployed in history, in order

to grasp both the originality and the difficulty of the existence of the 'civilization' that is seeking its place today.

The hunter-gatherers

In the beginning, hunter-gatherer societies offer the model of *societies simultaneously horizontal and religious.* Several concentric circles form their social world. The largest group is that of the tribe, which numbers between 500 and 2,500 people, adults and children included. The next largest group is that of the extended families, whose number oscillates between 30 and 50 people. It is between these two circles that the dense core of social relations is instituted, at the scale of the clan, which controls the hunting grounds and the religious rituals, such as the ceremonies connected with the transition to adulthood. This core is the incarnation of the unit of society. When the clan becomes too big, it splits into new clans that continue their adventure in different directions. The first humans migrate following their discovery of natural resources or game to be exploited. But they migrate also, and perhaps especially, because they do not allow themselves to cross a threshold beyond which their political organization would no longer hold together.

The sentimental image of societies without political intelligence, crushed by Dunbar's law setting the maximum number of direct relationships at 150, does not allow us, however, to understand the formidable political inventiveness of our ancestors. David Graeber and David Wengrow have written a luminous book warning against the idea according to which so-called 'primitive' societies all share a single form of egalitarian society, as if it were immutable in nature.[18] In reality, there exist as many hunter-gatherer societies that conform to a horizontal model as there are others in which hierarchies are strong. Thus, we find many examples of these societies dominated by a warrior aristocracy that held slaves, the latter

having been seized in razzias against rival tribes. The Upper
Palaeolithic, which covers the period that extends from
50,000 to 15,000 years before our era, created many princely
tombs, stone temples, imposing edifices, and monuments
constructed of mammoth bones, challenging the idea that the
first human societies were limited to small, egalitarian units.

To grasp the diversity of the situations encountered,
Graeber and Wengrow take their inspiration from the
work of the anthropologist Gregory Bateson, the founder
of the Palo Alto School. Bateson introduced the idea of
'schismogenesis' to characterize this specific tendency of
human societies to define themselves in opposition to one
another. The rivalry between Athens and Sparta is the perfect
example of this. Each of them is to the other what the sea is
to the land, cosmopolitanism to xenophobia, democracy to
oligarchy. This opposition is found in almost the same terms
on the Pacific coast of North America before the arrival of
European settlers. The societies of the Southwest resembled
the canonical egalitarian model. Exactly the opposite is
observed in the Northwest, in the region of the present-
day city of Vancouver. Society there was controlled by an
aristocracy that practised slavery. In a reversed, mirror
image, the 'California' group in the South did not know
slavery at all. It was profoundly peaceful, eating acorns
and pine nuts, even though salmon, which was the main
commodity in the North, was no less abundant in the South.

The most fascinating point bears on the ability of a society
to change its model as the seasons change. In 1944, Claude
Lévi-Strauss wrote an article about the Nambikwara, a small
group that lived on the savannah of Mato Grosso in Brazil.
During the dry season, which is also the hunting season, this
society adopts the Spartan customs of a military society.
Warrior chiefs gain ascendancy over the rest of the population
by manifesting an 'authoritarianism that would not have
been considered acceptable under any other circumstances'.

But as soon as the rainy season returned, bringing with it 'comfort and abundance', the society suddenly changed in nature. The warrior chiefs no longer controlled anything, and the renown they had acquired during the period of hunting was barely sufficient to allow them to take advantage of the goodwill of a few loyal followers.

Many examples attest to this seasonal nature of social relationships. Every time modern researchers discover sumptuous monuments arising from societies that were thought to be limited to the simplest expression, we can assume that they were constructed for the purpose of seasonal assemblies. Marcel Mauss and Henri Beuchat had published a study entitled *Seasonal Variations of the Eskimo: A Study in Social Morphology* that arrived at the same diagnosis. The same reversibility is found among the Native Americans of the Great Plains. The latter gave up their agricultural way of life and became nomads again after the arrival of the Europeans, domesticating the horses that had escaped from the encampments of the new occupants. During the period of the buffalo hunts, small groups of Cheyennes and Lakotas gathered in large congregations in accord with a very coercive model in which any offender could be whipped or imprisoned. But everything changed as soon as hunting season was over. After changing from the clan stage to the state stage in November, they returned to the egalitarian model when spring came. This seasonal nature of social life is still part of our existence, even though it is now only a shadow of itself. The period of so-called 'long holidays' in France reflects this powerful desire to change life in accord with the seasons.

Agrarian societies

Thanks to the works of archaeologists, it has been possible to date precisely the appearance of the first harvests in the 'Fertile Crescent' of the Middle East, about 12,000 years ago. It is usual to think that agriculture led to sedentary life. However, according to Jacques Cauvin, it seems possible that it might be the other way round.[19] In fact, it is far more plausible that it was the societies that were already sedentary that succeeded in understanding that a seed dropped in a field made a plant bloom there several months later.

Agriculture was to produce a second explosive shock: demographic growth. Whereas the fertility rate of women in hunter-gatherer societies was relatively low (because having to move around led to a natural limitation of births), agricultural societies experienced an exponential rise in their population. It was to be their curse. The 'law' attributed to Thomas Malthus was inexorably in force: the demographic explosion absorbed the surplus that agriculture had freed up. The agricultural revolution did not enable human beings to be better nourished, but it did enable them to become more numerous. After some time, abundance always gives way to famine. Quantity wins out over quality, the fundamental and emblematic example of humans' need to understand collectively the consequences of their individual acts.

About 300,000 years ago, when modern humans began their adventure, their population amounted to hundreds of thousands, at most a million. An initial break came between the year 40,000 and the year 30,000 BCE. The human population reached 4 or 5 million. Then, with the emergence of agriculture 12,000 years ago, a new trajectory began. The population surpassed 10 million when the great civilizations of the Middle East appeared, and then 100 million when the latter disappeared, around the year 1000 BCE. The human population then grew rapidly to reach 250 million at the beginning of the Common Era, a billion in 1800, 2 billion in 1930, and 8 billion today, and is projected to reach 10 billion in 2050.[20] Over the last 8 millennia, the world population began doubling every 1,000 years, then every century, and now every 50 years!

Since the invention of agriculture, the density of the human population has not ceased to grow, constantly pushing societies to the limits of their psychic and political balances, sweeping away the limits predicted by the Dunbar law. What are the social mechanisms that have made it possible to absorb such a demographic explosion? One of the solutions is the hierarchical model, which was one of the world's possibilities even before agriculture, but was soon to become the dominant form of social relations. Herbert Simon explains its logic perfectly. Starting from the average size of a clan, say 150 people, and assuming that each of these 150 people commanded 150 others who did the same, and so forth, spectacular levels of population can rapidly be managed. If there are 6 hierarchical levels (Milgram's figure), in which each node commands 150 people (Dunbar's figure), this suffices to create a society containing 76 billion humans! The ability to build such cathedrals is the amazing leap that hierarchical societies, for better and for worse, have enabled humanity to make.

For almost 10,000 years, these agrarian societies designed the social order from which we are just now emerging. The hierarchies that they constructed are not only techniques of organization, but a mentality whose greatest and most significant weight lies in the relation between the sexes. Pre-agrarian societies developed a variety of situations concerning women, not all of which were to their disadvantage.[21] Agriculture upset the relations between the sexes. A new social profile was established: men did outside work, women did inside work. Agrarian societies devalued women, limiting them to the role of reproductive agents.

Religion has been dying for a long time

The transformation of human hunter-gatherer societies into agricultural societies was accompanied by a radical transformation of their religious imagination. Yves Lambert, like Graeber and Wengrow, warns us against an excessively linear reading of the history of religions.[22] Many of them succeeded in adapting to the transformations of the world – like shamanism, for example. The idea that agriculture is automatically the cause of a change in religious practices has also been challenged by Jacques Cauvin, who has proposed an inversion of causality: as he sees it, the turmoil in religious beliefs preceded the invention of agriculture.[23]

Lambert has studied in detail the societies of Siberian hunters: not very dense, nomadic, without chiefs, and corresponding to the ideal type – egalitarian and small in size – of pre-agrarian societies. For these societies, everything involves 'immersion in nature, an exchange of life force between humans and animals', according to Lambert. The animal itself is put on an equal footing with humans: it is endowed with a soul and a life force equivalent to those of humans. Animals are supposed to be organized into clans, like humans. Hunting is understood as a reciprocal exchange in which the shaman is the mediator: 'People obtain game, negotiated in advance with the animal spirits, through the agency of the shaman; in return, animals take some of humans' life force: disease, old age, and death are the price of the game taken.'

These shamanic beliefs are also found among the Inuits, the Pygmies, the Bushmen, and the Australian Aborigines. For these societies, it is inconceivable to eat animals that have been domesticated. The only game that can be eaten is game that has been hunted. Religious life involves neither prayer nor sacrifice. For Alain Testart, there is an absolute absence of hierarchical relations between humans and with regard to gods. 'Humans are not considered inferior to a class of beings that are called gods elsewhere. Neither are they superior to another class of dependent and inferior beings whose life it would be legitimate to take to offer it to the gods.' Here we have the typical case of a society that is at once egalitarian and religious, the first type in our classification.

The evolution towards livestock-raising and agriculture radically upset all these beliefs. It gave humans an unprecedented feeling of superiority to animals. Respect is henceforth focused on the ancestors to whom humans are obligated for having created the world as it is. Whereas shamanic societies do not hesitate to abandon elderly people whose 'life force' is declining, cultivators' societies place the cult of the old at the summit of their values. The world was no longer classified in accord with the ability to hunt, but in accord with the seniority of the chiefs. The farmer asks the heavens for rain and peace. Agricultural societies engaged in a practice of prayer and sacrifice that was unknown to hunter-gatherer societies.

This religious consciousness tended to be brought under the control of the state, with the appearance of the great ancient civilizations in Egypt and Mesopotamia, on the banks of the Indus and the Ganges, or in the Andes, on the Pacific coast. There was a transition from an oral, agrarian religion to a polytheistic, state religion, with monumental temples and complex liturgies. 'As society became hierarchical, it tended to hierarchize its image', writes Jean Bottéro.[24] We are at the heart of the process that would lead to the second type of human society: vertical and religious. Animal sacrifices become more numerous, food is presented to the gods and ends up on the tables of the priests, who become a specialized, often hereditary, caste. Writing also helps to strengthen priestly power. Bringing the clergy under state control creates a separation between the official religion and the popular religion. A silent gap thus opens up between the official practice of religion, which magnifies the emperor (who is, along with a few high dignitaries, the only mortal promised immortality), and the religion of the people, who retain some of the forms of the earlier oral religions founded on the cult of ancestors.

For Karl Jaspers, a new de-centring of the religious world takes place in the short period of time between 600 and 200

BCE, during which religions shifted towards a new system in which individual ethics occupied an unprecedented place. This is the change of model that was proposed by Confucius and Lao Tse in China, the Buddha in India, Zoroaster in Iran, the prophets in Israel, and Homer and Socrates in Greece. The unity that previously existed between the cosmos, the social order, and human well-being was stretched. For Jaspers, this is the moment at which humanity wakes up to itself. Human societies are no longer defined by their heritage, that of the great ancestors, human or divine, but by the ethical rules that humans assign to themselves. Happiness no longer consists in accepting nature as it is, but rather in humans' ability to give themselves their own criteria of existence.

The conditions under which these religions appear are similar. They were all born in periods of troubles in which the old powers were faltering. Confucius came into the world in the 'Warring States' period, when the fall of the Zhou dynasty opened a cycle of conflicts under different lords. To restore order, Confucius founded a new ethics, that of the good man who goes from being a good father to being a just sovereign who turns away from the chaotic violence of the aristocracy. The prophets of Israel began to write the Bible in the chaos provoked by the destruction of the Temple and their Babylonian exile.[25] The Greek miracle was born on the basis of ravaging wars between the city-states, under the threat of the Persian Empire. Religions became aware that civilizations can perish. The connection between religion and the state was rethought. Buddhist monks and students in yeshivas explored new ways of being fully human: they foresaw what Louis Dumont was to call the 'individual outside the world', which, according to him, prefigures contemporary individualism.

However, we should not be misled by traits of these religions that we would today call philosophical: they remain haunted by the presence of the gods. These are religions of salvation that democratized above all the promise of eternal life, which was formerly reserved for the pharaohs and other emperors. Even though they arose in a period when the great empires of the past were in decline, curiously enough, along with Christianity in Rome and Confucianism in China, they fed a reinvention of the imperial idea. For all that, the worm was in the fruit: the religious world and the political world were no longer perfectly aligned with one another.

In Europe, with the fall of the Roman Empire, two powers, two concurrent systems of values, fought over the government of souls: the ecclesiastical power and the aristocratic power. The former preached the equality of all humans before God, the latter preached the exact opposite. As the sociologist Philippe d'Iribane says, this contradiction is particularly intense in France, which pushes very high the level of hypocrisy necessary to resolve it, where everyone is equal in church but ceases to be equal the moment they leave it. It is this duality of the feudal world that was to be transformed by the modern times that began in the fifteenth century.

This upheaval foreshadows the world in which we still live.

The Secular Age

Ecclesiastical values were challenged by the scientific revolution ignited by Descartes and Galileo. The latter said that to decipher God's work, it sufficed to change the alphabet, using mathematics rather than Latin. The Cartesian *cogito* – the manifesto of a modernity in which the heroic human stands alone facing heavens that have become empty – is the logical conclusion of these evolutions of the religious psyche. The philosopher Charles Taylor has vividly described how modern times were going to give rise to what he calls the 'secular age', this new world that is still ours, and within which religion, without disappearing, is now no more than one way, among many others, of living.[26]

The rise of absolutist states, from the fifteenth century on, also transformed aristocratic values. The control of a feudal aristocracy was the principal stake in the transformations that monarchy imprinted. Aristocrats were snatched up by a court society that changed the valiant warriors they were into servants of the royal power. Instead of fighting, nobles had to read Castiglione's *Book of the Courtier*, which would teach them the art of respecting increasingly strict social rules. As the sociologist Norbert Elias shows, the royal court became the seat of radical transformations in matters of morals and privacy. The courtier had to rigorously control his rage, violence, and resentment. It gradually became unsuitable to use the tablecloth when blowing one's nose, or to defecate in public places, even if the king himself remained surrounded by his courtiers when he sat on the 'chaise percée'! The requirements of refinement thus allowed the aristocracy to differentiate itself socially from the rising bourgeoisie that nonetheless rapidly imitated it, or tried to, like Molière's M. Jourdain.

But it was in fact the bourgeoisie that was to have the last word, and that, as Marx would say, 'ultimately drowned the most heavenly ecstasies of religious fervour, of chivalrous enthusiasm, of Philistine sentimentalism, in the icy water of egotistical calculation'. Albert Hirschman wrote a book that has become a classic for understanding how the love of glory, still described by Corneille as the sole reason to live, was to gradually give way to a different passion: 'cupidity', renamed 'self-interest' for the needs of the modern world. The shift towards the bourgeois mentality can be interpreted as the passage from one passion, that of heroism, to another, that of profit, which is just as intense as the preceding ones, but which is praised by its sycophants for having the virtue of being able to engender order and stability. Cupidity is a 'compensatory passion': it checks others. Spinoza had a premonition about this mutation when he wrote that 'a feeling can be opposed or suppressed only by a feeling that is contrary to it and stronger than the feeling to be opposed'. The love of profit has the merit, in the eyes of the bourgeois morality, of being predictable. That is the argument that inspired Adam Smith when he explained that it was better to depend on his baker's self-interest than on his goodwill.

Social control that extends to the population as a whole was, however, exercised in a much rougher way than the theorists of the market suggest. As Charles Taylor reminds us, referring to the works of Michel Foucault, modern times invented a new disciplinary system in which delinquents, the mad, and the poor are driven out of the public space. Charity, which had earlier been unconditional, became much more severe: now the poor had to work in order to deserve it. The breath of fresh air represented by carnivals was gradually prohibited. In 1503, Erasmus, who was one of the authors who made 'civility' a new imperative, accused carnival of not being Christian, of bearing the traces of old-fashioned paganism. During the carnival, everything became possible. Women could act like men, children could command adults, servants could make their masters slave away, ancestors could return from the dead, and kings could be crowned and then dethroned.

Michel Foucault's books, from *The History of Madness* to *Discipline and Punish*, passing by way of *The Birth of the Clinic*, meticulously describe the process which, with varying intensity, was to characterize a new ideal type of social organization – that of 'disciplinary societies'. Foucault devotes a famous passage of *Discipline and Punish* to the description of Jeremy Bentham's 'panopticon', in which the founder of utilitarianism explains how a model prison has to make it possible to monitor, from an ideal observation post, all of the prisoners in their cells. The moral perfection of the

kind of self-control that the elites must impose on themselves
has, as its flipside, a relentless discipline forced upon those
at the bottom of the social ladder by the central authority.

The industrial mentality

It was in this amazing disorder of values that the world of
which we are the direct heirs was born. All through the eighteenth century, the Enlightenment sought to translate into a
secular language the idea of divine providence, by making it
part of a new promise, that of progress. Enlightenment also
exported, in the political domain, the idea of sovereignty, by
transferring its depository from the royal government to the
people. Via Adam Smith, a friend and continuer of David
Hume, the idea of nature was then transferred to the sphere of
markets. Smith theorizes the idea that there are 'natural' prices
towards which current prices 'gravitate' in accord with laws
to which the sovereign himself must submit, as he does to the
laws of nature. These ideas are at the heart of a secular way
of thought that forged the horizon of the nineteenth century.

But the Industrial Revolution also inherited the disciplinary model that had been established in order to control
the plebs. Factories, schools, and hospitals became places
where collective life was put under surveillance. The factory
and the school were certainly not invented in the nineteenth
century. Factories had existed since time immemorial (slave
labour existed in factories in Antiquity, and was passed
down to us by way of Colbert's porcelain factories). But
pre-industrial labour took place chiefly in the countryside,
in what has been called a kind of 'protocapitalism'. At
that time, the capitalist limited himself to bringing the raw
materials to the worker's home and picking up the finished
work, paid for by the piece. The way the nineteenth century
industrialized social life took a new turn by closing up
workers in confined places.

The breakaway from the agrarian world towards the industrial one marks above all the transition from a religious order to a secular order. People believed in God, now they believe in Reason. Engineers replace priests. However, this mutation remains inscribed in a profoundly hierarchical conception of society. The chain of command that goes from the CEO and the engineer to the factory worker, by way of the foreman, is as strict as the one that used to go from the king to his barons and from the latter to their peasants. The authorities, who had been religious, became secular, but the Enlightenment's ideal of emancipation was broken, each individual being still assigned to a fixed place in a new order just as inegalitarian as the preceding one. Industrial societies have constructed the third type of social relations: *secular and hierarchical*.

The sixties

It is only with the passage to a post-industrial society, in the sixties, that the humanist aspirations born with the Enlightenment started to become a new political imperative. Self-expression, as the sociologist Ronald Ingelhart put it, became the founding element of a society centred on individual development. Mass education offers everyone the intellectual means to have an independent mind. The welfare state cuts the tie of material dependency between children and parents. Of necessity, communities are transformed into 'elective affinities'. Education, urbanization, democratization, and the turning upside down of the relations of domination between men and women: everything contributes to the development of a society of autonomy and tolerance. Thus, post-industrial society promotes the return of the Enlightenment ideal of a society consisting of autonomous subjects, freed from the old agrarian order. That is the hope borne by the counterculture of the 1960s.

In the sixties, the hierarchical conception of society became unacceptable in factories as well as in families and schools. For the sociologist Daniel Bell, this protest is itself the result of what he designated as 'capitalism's cultural contradictions'. Capitalism, he explains, is permeated by a permanent tension between the sphere of production, which is haunted by an ideal of order and renunciation, on the one hand, and, on the other, the ideal of consumption, marketing, and advertising, which offers images 'of glamour and sex, and promotes a hedonistic way of life'. One urges obedience, the other debauchery.

As Bell sees them, these 'cultural contradictions' inherit tensions internal to the bourgeoisie itself, torn between its requirements of 'calculation and order' and its Faustian appetite for boundless wealth. It constantly revolutionizes the processes of production and consumption, attempting to reconcile the moral order on which its fundamental values depend – the values of property and authority – with the economic disorder it generates itself. There comes a time when these two dimensions can no longer cohabit. The cultural revolution of the 1960s is the moment when this equilibrium is broken, when young people, infatuated with freedom and autonomy, reject the world that has been handed down to them.

Yet, instead of the promised world of equality, the sixties hastened Reagan's and Thatcher's conservative revolution. The period that began in the 1980s was fed by the idea that society existed, as Thatcher put it, only as a collection of lonely agents interacting through the mediation of markets.

It was the era when Milton Friedman's views triumphed, demolishing the idea of the enterprise as a social habitat in favour of the idea according to which the directors of these firms had to serve exclusively their owners.[27] The book *Markets and Hierarchies* by Oliver Williamson, Nobel Prize-winner in Economics, shed light on the terms of the alternative as they could be seen at the time. We have to choose between a world of 'organizations', where hierarchies are the rule, and another world ruled by the market and competition. For these authors, there seems to be no third option.

In many respects, the digital revolution inherited both from the eighties and the sixties. It spurred competition between producers, giving enterprises new ways to externalize and offshore production and reduce their costs. But it also inherits the spirit of the sixties and seventies. The American college campuses where protest against the Vietnam War and bourgeois morality had been strongest were now the pioneers of the digital world that was emerging. The digital revolution was directly claimed by this counterculture and its open-source egalitarian model.

Something unprecedented in human history then became conceivable: the outline of an egalitarian society that believed only in itself, without any transcendent authority, religious or secular. It discovered a continent that up to that time had never been explored by human civilizations, the last possible model: *horizontal and secular.*

The Triumph of Endogamy

The invention of Fordism in the early twentieth century profoundly transformed the imagination of its period. It was at the heart of the dense industrial world it created that the labour movement flourished. White- and blue-collar workers lived in the same world, in a tightly hierarchical model. This system had one merit, however: it was inclusive. Salary increases for the top management 'trickled down' to production workers, because of unions and the simple fact that all employees were connected to one another by the same salary grids. In the new system that was installed in the 1980s, everything was turned upside down. High-skilled workers were regrouped together, as were low-skilled workers.

A study on the rise of inequalities in America has shown that their explosion in the last thirty years is closely connected with this process.[28] Whereas the differences in income between the extremes have returned to the levels of the nineteenth century, wiping out in a few decades the astonishing compression that had been observed in the twentieth century, inequalities within enterprises themselves have hardly changed at all. It is the inequalities between companies that have exploded. The new atomization of the personnel into so many separate worlds no longer produces an equalization of wealth. The 'trickle-down' of wealth announced by Reagan and Thatcher has been scientifically blocked since the beginning of the 1980s by this orchestration of social distanciation.

Being with one's own kind

However, despite growing inequalities, each firm became more egalitarian, relative to the rest of the society. Within firms employing high-skilled or low-skilled workers, a more horizontal society emerged, in which, for instance, the use of familiar forms of address (e.g., first names rather than 'Mr X') became the rule, though only in small groups. Reciprocity and trust are indeed present, but no attention is paid to other strata of society.

One of the terms that is sometimes used to describe this way of living together is 'homophilia'. This expression was used in 1974 by Paul Lazarsfeld and Robert Merton, two famous American sociologists, to characterize the propensities of each social group to gather together. Their analysis showed this tendency at work in circles of friends, neighbourhoods, and athletic clubs, in all the possible sociological dimensions: religions, age groups, occupations, levels of education, etc. But the term 'homophilia' is misleading. It gives the impression that every stratum of society aspires to stay together, whereas very often it is social segregation that closes each group in on itself. If poor people are crammed into the same urban ghettos, it is certainly not out of the desire to stay together, but rather because they have no other choice. If the children of advantaged social groups are found in classes where they encounter only their peers, that is because their parents' social strategy leads them there. As is shown by the works of Pierre-André Chiappori, couples are more and more 'well-matched' because of the growing importance that parents assign to their children's education.[29] Educated women marry educated men in order to maximize the chances of their offspring's success at school. That leaves women with average educations no choice other than to marry someone with the same level of education, and so on until the bottom of the social ladder is reached. The term 'social endogamy' is much better suited to describing the current process.

The spontaneous tendency of social classes to be parked in their respective ghettos is certainly not new, but what is troubling about it is the speed with which it has accelerated. In 1970, two Americans out of three lived in 'middle-class' neighbourhoods. In 2009, less than two people out of five lived in a neighbourhood where the average income was close to the national average. Even independently of social networks, it is on this soil of a growing segregation of society that distrust has been growing.

Alberto Alesina and Katya Zhuravskaya showed, by studying ethnic rivalries in various countries, how segregation also increases distrust of others and of public institutions. These authors distinguished two types of situations. In a first group of countries, ethnic diversity is uniformly distributed over the whole of the territory: for instance, in each region there is the same percentage of populations of the blue or the red type. In the other group, they find a very marked regional differentiation: the blues and the reds each live 'with their own kind' in very distinct regions. The study concludes without ambiguity that the second type, the one in which segregation prevails, produces a much stronger distrust across groups. Everyone lives with the fantasy of a rivalry that can degenerate into civil war. Political parties often throw oil on the fire to retain their troops. Another study by Banerjee and Pande has shown that the battle for the ethnic vote is one of the reasons for the poor quality of public institutions, which are corrupted and eaten away by clientelism.[30]

The central paradox of the contemporary world can thus be summed up as follows: life with one's peers is becoming the rule, fulfilling in a narrow manner the promise of horizontality that was sought in the 1960s. As a result, global inequalities are growing explosively, with no reactive force still connecting the different social strata as the great industrial enterprises used to do. In the domain of mentalities, a perverse loop begins to operate between the ghettoization of society and a general distrust of other people. The latter is not directly caused by social networks: it is the result of major forces that begin to take effect long before they become manifest. But, far from building bridges between communities, they give a deafening echo to public distrust, pushing to the extreme the impossibility of communication between different social groups. The fact that universalist values lose ground when social groups live apart from one another should not come as much of a surprise. Yet the criticism of Enlightenment ideas rose partly from within Western values themselves. This could be seen as a postmodern moment that social networks have embraced in their own way.

The Postmodern Mentality

Postmodern theories had a foundational moment with the publication in 1979 of Jean-François Lyotard's book

La Condition postmoderne: rapport sur le savoir (*The Postmodern Condition: A Report on Knowledge*, trans. G. Bennington, 1984). Lyotard interpreted our age as the one that marks the exhaustion of the great myths that had borne the modern world, those of the French Revolution or of sexual emancipation, in which humans had become 'the heroic agents of their own liberation'. The postmodern mentality prospers amid the ruins of the 'great narratives' that have structured modernity. The age in which the hero seeks the truth gives way to disbelief. Universalism fades, making room for a plurality of languages – scientific, political, cultural – where the heterogeneity of discourses becomes the rule. Where can the legitimacy of a discourse of truth reside? In discussion and debate, as the philosopher Jürgen Habermas thinks? This presupposes that the problem is resolved – namely, that everyone agrees on the possibility of an agreement between reasonable minds. For Lyotard, this Enlightenment moment has passed and nothing can be done about it: we have to admit the multiplicities of 'meta-argumentations'.

Taking up these themes again, Fredric Jameson inter-preted postmodernism as the spirit of a 'late capitalism'.[31] When society is saturated with consumer goods, nothing remains but to 'aestheticize' them: make cars or televisions more elegant, more baroque, in order to keep the flame burning. Nostalgia for the 'heroic' period when access to new goods embodied the idea of progress made way for a capitalism that was more obsessed with advertising than with production. The postmodern moment, according to Jameson, incarnates the stage when capitalism turns away from material goods in order to produce, above all, individual and collective fantasies. We enjoy our ability to simulate alternative societies, without having to pay the cost of really experiencing them. In postmodernism, 'the true becomes an element of the false', as Guy Debord already stated in *Society of the Spectacle* (1967). Within this world where nature has disappeared, the apocalypse itself now appears as 'a decorative element'.[32]

Jameson interprets postmodernity as the moment when culture triumphs definitively over nature. Modernity was itself a moment when realities emerging from radically different periods of history continued to coexist. We find artisans surviving in the midst of the cartels of heavy industry, peasants' fields adjoining modern factories. Kafka, for example, is the expression of a hiatus between the modern world and an obsolete imperial bureaucracy. In the postmodern era, this survival of archaic forms of existence is swept away. Culture rules, with little reference to nature.

In praise of archaism

It is difficult to resist drawing the conclusion that digital society embodies this postmodern mentality. The appearance of a post- (fake) truth in which each individual cultivates his own 'meta-discourse' is perfectly coherent with what is happening on social networks. In a world limited to the like-minded, universalism fades away. To break these centrifugal forces in society, the first thing to do is surely to avoid burying too quickly the 'archaic' forms that used to produce social cohesion, whether these are labour unions, political parties, or businesses themselves. To maintain or reinvent the role of these actors, the tasks to be accomplished are immense. Several volumes would not suffice to list them all, but the general line is clear: contrary to the ideas developed in the 1980s, we can never emphasize enough the fact that the enterprise is a place of shared lives, that labour unions are essential for their regulation, that the 'gig economy' must be subject to social welfare law,[33] that democratic life needs political parties, and that truth needs scientists!

Obviously, this does not mean that there is no need to reflect on the tools that the digital offers us. For starters, we would like the contemporary society of surveillance to be exercised more on business enterprises than on individuals.[34] Thus we can think about generalizing the environmental and social rating of enterprises, and about making, for example, an A rating mandatory to gain access to public spending. This A rating would require not only that the firm itself be high-ranking on economic and social standards, but also – and especially – that its sub-contractors be A-rated too, which would mean that these sub-contractors' sub-contractors would also have to be A-rated, and so on. It would therefore no longer be possible to externalize social problems. Clearly, this is only one small part of the problem, but it shows how the power of digital society could be put in the service of social cohesion. It is by rediscovering the new social geography, between social groups, enterprises, and territories, that the means of creating a new, inclusive model is to be found.

Ideas of the same kind could be put in place to check post-truth. To track down 'fake news', strengthened press agencies should have the means to certify information sites. One site might thus be of A or B quality, depending on the sources that it puts into circulation. For instance, information would be A-rated if it originates from sources (newspapers or books) with a managing editor (answerable for the information published) publication. Every user of B news would immediately be warned that no one stands behind it. We must also reflect on the means of protecting individuals from digital harassment. A site that publishes appeals to hatred or to murder must be held responsible for them.

Reflecting on political life is just as indispensable. To use Michel Offerlé's expression, the French presidential election now consists of 'a leader and the Internet', and reduces democracy to a blank cheque given every five years to a single person, which is becoming completely suffo-cating. A reflection specific to France regarding the limits of presidentialism is necessary, but the question extends in fact to all democratic countries. Voters demand horizontality in political life as well as in social life, but they end up despising politics at large because they feel they are not heard.

Whatever the remedies to be used, we see the central paradox of digital society emerging.

It gives rise to an aspiration to open discussion, but proves incapable of organizing the necessary confrontation of opposite ideas. It keeps the desire for a horizontal, secular society alive, but it does so by imprisoning each social stratum in a silo of its own. The eclipse of intermediary bodies, political parties or labour unions, if it were to continue its present course, would deprive the digital world of the means to construct an inclusive society. It is only by seeking to make these two requirements – horizontality and cohesion – compatible that digital tools can become useful.

6

Winter Is Coming

The Crises of the Twenty-First Century

In spring 2020, ducks were seen at the Comédie Française, jaguars in Santiago de Chile, and elephants walked freely about in Mumbai. Work stopped in Paris, New York, London, and Milan. 'Like an organism put under anaesthesia, the economy no long performed its vital functions', wrote INSEE to characterize the month of April 2020. Covid plunged us into Will Smith's film *I Am Legend* or Charlton Heston's *The Omega Man*. In both cases, the hero is the only survivor of a health crisis that has destroyed humanity.

For the postmodern, post-truth mentality, the shock was devastating. So a real world did actually exist, with epidemics and wars, and human beings 'truly' lived in it! Trump could argue that Covid was just another flu – it was not. Covid elicited existential uncertainties that modern societies had become unaccustomed to talking about in public: life, death, concern about other people. It was not a matter of coping with a 'technical' crisis like a computer bug or the failure of a bank. It was a 'total social fact', to paraphrase Marcel Mauss. It tested the cohesion of the whole society, involving registers fundamentally different from earlier crises. Even the language used to describe the crisis constantly evolved. People talked about a war economy, and then about solidarity. The organization of the public space was turned upside down. The state had to take responsibility for crucial vocational and family decisions (sending children to school or not). Yet it quickly appeared that managing the crisis required co-production by the state with all the social actors involved: households, businesses, and healthcare personnel.

Resilience when confronted by the virus was closely linked to people's confidence in their public institutions, whether they were of the government or the scientific community.[1] Horizontal confidence, that of individuals with regard to other people, and vertical confidence, that of citizens with regard to public authorities, each played a crucial role. The stronger horizontal confidence was, the weaker the legal prohibitions were. In Sweden, where interpersonal confidence is among the highest anywhere in the world, public restrictions were minimal. France, where interpersonal confidence is weak, weathered the first lockdown relatively well, for a reason symmetrical with that in Sweden: the French expected the state to protect them against the supposed weak public-spiritedness of their fellow citizens.

Lockdown highlighted the importance of the connections that hold a society together: meeting co-workers on the job, friends in a café, or fellow students at school. Despite the desire to meet with other people, working from home has nonetheless become, after the lockdown, something to which almost everyone aspired. Beyond the discovery of technical solutions implemented during the crisis, Zoom, Teams, and other video-conferencing programs have been established in people's minds as an alternative, even if only partial, to regular work. As Paul Krugman puts it, for many employees the pandemic was an opportunity to reflect on their personal situation. 'Many people who have been able to work from home have realized how much they hated commuting. Some who worked in the hotel and restaurant industry realized, during their months of involuntary unemployment, how much they hated their jobs.' A significant number of employees decided not to go back to their old jobs. Americans talk about the 'great resignation' to describe the post-Covid crisis. It is in this context that work from home appeared to some people as a space of freedom. The temptations of digital society, of living, thanks to working from home, without the constraints of ordinary occupational life, proved to be stronger.

The virus was also the theatre of a silent battle between the two sides of the contemporary world, China and the United States. During the first lockdown, 'Confucian' values and the respect for public health restrictions in Asian countries made Western countries, which had proved incapable of implementing the apparently effective test–isolate–trace system, green with envy. In contrast, the United States, led by a Trump who had become an adept of post-truth, registered far higher mortality rates. However, with the discovery of vaccines, the honours list was inverted, and China's 'zero Covid' policy became extremely costly. Shanghai was completely immobilized, despite the vehement protests of a population forced to remain holed up at home, whatever difficulties they might encounter simply to feed themselves. At the paroxysm of the digital dystopia seen from China, robotic dogs were used to impose the curfew. Trump could gloat: the vaccines brought order to the disorder he had created. Schumpeterian values, those of innovation, won out over those of Confucius.

Vaccines and anti-vaxxers

Nevertheless, the West had to confront an internal enemy: anti-vaxxers, strengthened by their own networks. Even before the public health crisis, they had constructed a separate world, feeding on fake news that claimed that the MMR vaccine (measles, mumps, rubella) caused autism in children. This idea had been clearly refuted by the scientific community; the author of the article who claimed to have established it was struck off the register of British physicians and forbidden to practise medicine. That did not prevent his claim from circulating widely on social networks.

To what point can one deny reality in the name of one's fantasies? Covid was a life-size test of the power of the reality principle in a post-truth world. Between the adolescent who is afraid of shots and Trumpers who challenge the very principle of state regulation, via the tennis player Novak Djokovic, who has a mystical relation to his body, the variations are in reality considerable. Trumpers have been the most vehement, making the refusal to be vaccinated a political cause, going as far as one can in denying the scientific evidence. The polarization of the United States explains why this country, which had begun its vaccination programme with great ado in early 2021, after Biden's inauguration as president, ended up falling behind other rich countries. A study on France showed that the communes in which the rate of vaccination was lowest were also those in which participation in politics was lowest (taking into account the other characteristics of the latter, especially age and population density). Rejection of vaccines was in fact related to a more general abandonment of public life.

During the first phase of the crisis, France was also characterized by an abrupt decline in trust in the scientific community.[2] What experts said was devalued, and their hesitations as the crisis evolved were seen as a mark of weakness.[3] According to inquiries conducted in early 2021, more than 45 per cent of French people did not want to be vaccinated, a figure that was initially comparable to that in the United States. Nevertheless, France succeeded in overcoming its anti-vaccine handicap, especially after the implementation of a vaccine pass in July 2021. A fascinating study by Mathias Dewatripont notes, however, that the same dynamic has been observed in Spain, where the vaccine pass was, however, rejected by the courts.[4] The star student in the European class was Portugal, Italy achieving a grade equal to that of France. Conversely, the countries seen as respecting public order, Germany and the Netherlands, long lagged behind the countries of southern Europe. The trauma of the initial health shock to public health served in fact as the main driving force behind vaccination, a proof that the real world does have an impact on people's consciousness, at least when there is an exit option. The problem, if we think about the coming climate challenges, is that this impact occurs only after the crisis has struck, never in a preventive way.

The age of catastrophes

'*A fame, bello et peste, libera nos Domine*' ('From hunger, war, and pestilence, deliver us, O Lord'). This fourteenth-century prayer has reverberated strangely among our contemporaries. Europeans had hardly begun to emerge from the modern plague of Covid than they entered, with Ukraine, into war and hunger (for wheat, oil, and gas). In the Middle Ages, the crisis of the fourteenth century annihilated the feudal system, and the Renaissance was able to come after it. We would like to tell ourselves that crises accelerate the march of History, that Covid made possible the discovery of revolutionary vaccines, and that the war in Ukraine will demonstrate the futility of wars in the twenty-first century. But how can we be sure about that?

The war in Ukraine is typical of these catastrophes that Europeans did not want to see and that, nonetheless, appear, retrospectively, to be unavoidable. The way in which the very possibility of war has been denied clearly shows that our beliefs are not a way of understanding the world, but a way of fabricating it. Europeans have believed in peace not in an objective manner, but rather to preserve their comfort zone. Henri Bergson, quoted by Jean-Pierre Dupuy in his book *Pour un catastrophisme éclairé*, said exactly the same thing about World War I. It was, according to Bergson, seen as simultaneously 'probable and impossible'. The Ukrainian crisis could not be better described. No one wanted to believe in it, even though it was moving forward in full view of the international community. Russian soldiers being massed on the borders meant nothing! American warnings were out of place! And then the catastrophe began. Everything became clear. The same line of argument that made war improbable made it inevitable in retrospect.

However, the war didn't happen as it was supposed to. Putin surprised the world by invading Ukraine, but the people of Ukraine also stupefied observers by not throwing down their arms, making it impossible for the international community, faced with so much heroism, to tergiversate regarding the aid to be given to it. This 'grain of sand' constituted by Ukrainian heroism changed the dynamics of events. It is this lesson in courage that must inspire the world in facing the catastrophes that are looming and that we refuse to see right in front of us.

The Climatic Clock

The great catastrophe of the twenty-first century, which is foreseeable, obvious, and yet irrepressible, is the climatic shock. However, no warning issued by experts had sufficed, for so many years, to convince people to act. It took a series of scorching summers, threatening forest fires, and photos of polar bears trying to find an ice floe before the climatic menace was taken seriously. Human beings have to 'feel' things to decide to act.

The disconnect between the perception of the world and its reality explains why humans act only on the brink of catastrophes. In the meantime, CO_2 is filling the atmosphere the way water fills a bathtub. It hardly matters whether it was emitted a century or a week ago: what counts for the climate is the overall quantity that has been accumulated over time. Forests and oceans capture a (small) part of what has been emitted, but despite these leaks, the climatic bathtub is irresistibly filling up. There comes a time when it will overflow. According to the estimates of the Intergovernmental Panel on Climate Change (IPPC), 85 per cent of our carbon budget has already been consumed. To gauge the speed with which it is filling, since 1990 we have emitted almost as much CO_2 (40 per cent of the total) as was emitted between 1850 and 1989![5] According to the IPPC report issued in April 2022, if we fail to reverse the current tendency before 2025, the bathtub will overflow! Then we would be irremediably headed for a global warming of over 1.5 per cent. The rise in temperatures is already 1.09 °C above pre-industrial values, heat waves are more intense each summer, forest fires and precipitation are increasing, and sea level is rising.[6]

In report after report, the IPPC warns against the risks that global warming entails for life on Earth. Increased desertification, the rarefaction of available bodies of water combined with the danger of new floods are the plagues on the horizon. Between 3.3 and 3.6 billion people live in an environment vulnerable to warming. Half of the species monitored are moving north or to higher altitudes to escape the heat, leading to an increase in transmissible diseases in regions such as the high plateaus of Africa, which were protected by a temperate climate. Southern Europe is also said to be particularly affected. More than a third of the population could be threatened there by water shortages. In France, the South might experience extreme temperatures during the summer, higher than 35 °C on twenty to thirty days a year. Tiger mosquitos (*aedes albopictus*) will multiply.

Even assuming that governments actually implement the measures they have announced, global warming could reach 2.8 °C before the end of the century. The IPPC has given, in its report for April 2022, the list of steps that have to be taken to avoid catastrophe. We must urgently transform our energy model, shifting to renewable energies.[7] We also have to radically change our nutritional habits to eat more vegetables, turn our means of transportation upside down by giving priority to trains, and consequently rethink the organization of space.[8] The transition will also, and perhaps especially, require profound reflections on global inequalities. The richest 10% of countries alone emit 40% of the world's CO_2 pollution, of which two-thirds comes from rich countries. The poorest 50% emit only 13% of the CO_2, less than the richest 1%. For example, an Afghan emits 1 ton a year, while a Frenchman emits about ten times more (including the emissions produced on his behalf in other countries).

Collapse

What prevents humans from acting? The standard book for understanding the logic of denial and stupor as we confront ecological crises is Jared Diamond's *Collapse*. This author, who has an insatiable curiosity, has meticulously described the way in which numerous civilizations – Easter Island, the Mayas, the Vikings – collapsed under the impact of ecological crises that they were not able to check. All of them were devoured by their internal rivalries and their inability to admit weaknesses in their civilizations.

The series *Game of Thrones* is a marvellous presentation in images of this apocalyptic risk. It was one of the great successes of the new world of TV series. 'Winter is coming' is the iconic expression that runs through the various episodes. The looming winter is not one season among others, but a glacial mini-age, an inverted metaphor of the climatic danger. The series makes this danger palpable, so to speak, by the fact that winter provokes the awakening of an army of the living dead, the Whitwalkers, which has arisen in the Great North, ready to invade the kingdom. As in the true history of Easter Island, rivalries among pretenders to the throne make the warlords totally insensitive to the impending danger. One after the other, the principal characters in the series, the better ones and the most perverse ones, are assassinated, in a dance that leaves no hope of a final happy ending. The hero, Jon Snow, is a reincarnated Christ. He is assassinated, then resuscitated to fulfil his 'mission'. In the last episode, which concludes eight years of unbearable waiting for the television audience, he has to go into exile in the Great North, which has become habitable again: there he will find true freedom.

This story indicates exactly where evil comes from. It is the rivalry among humans that prevents them from becoming collectively aware of the danger. The inhabitants of Easter Island needed a Jon Snow who was capable of offering himself as a sacrificial victim to alert them to the apocalyptic risks that were threatening them. But would it suffice to alert them, from the height of his cross, to the danger, to turn them away from their lethal course?

Collapsology

A bestselling book, *How Everything Can Collapse: A Manual for Our Times*, provided collapse with its theoretical manifesto.[9] Its authors resumed and updated the premonitory analysis produced in 1972 by a team at MIT, the 'Meadows Report'. Quickly translated into numerous languages, this report stated that the exhaustion of non-renewable resources would force industrial societies to make a major correction to their trajectory. The MIT book offered an extensive analysis of the growing human footprint on soil, water, and forests. It also owed a large measure of its success to the foreseeable end of fossil fuel energy, which made it, retrospectively, the harbinger of the oil crises of the 1970s. As we are learning today, however, the problem is not the scarcity of fossil fuels. In fact, it is the precise opposite: their abundance. It is the excess of such fuels that is endangering the terrestrial ecosystem. If we decided to use all the discoveries of oil, we would emit twenty-five times more CO_2 than our carbon budget allows.

However, as Servigne and Stevens show, the central message of the Meadows Report is still urgently relevant for all the other problems it examines. They remind us first of the mad race of our energy expenditures. During the twentieth century alone, on the planetary scale, energy consumption has increased by a factor of 10, the extraction of industrial materials by 27, and that of construction materials by 34. Other calamities would occur with the rise in sea level. Bangladesh is one of the countries from which the largest number of climate refugees might come: the southern third of the country could be drowned under the waves. The world's great deltas, in Egypt, Vietnam, or West Africa, are also in danger.

Will modern societies be able to stop before they reach the abyss? As Georges Bataille said in his book *The Accursed Share*, societies always tend to go all the way to the end of their possibilities. Civilizations that have succeeded in limiting themselves to avoid a collapse are in fact very rare. The example Diamond gives is that of a tiny island in the Pacific, Tikopia, where the inhabitants survived for 3,000 years at the limits of their forest economy. That is not very reassuring. Servigne and Stevens give a long list of reasons explaining the general denial of ecological crises, yesterday and today. It is disconcerting to note that the emotional forces at play are exactly those that are stimulated by social networks.

The first explanation is the predominance of Kahneman's 'system 1' in our thought. Our brains perform very well for dealing with immediate problems, but are very uncomfortable with long-term thinking. Dan Gilbert, a psychologist at Harvard, ironically summed things up this way: 'Many ecologists say that climate change is too rapid. In fact, it is too slow, it doesn't come fast enough to capture our attention!'

The second explanation, which is close to the preceding one, is the effect known as 'habituation'. We get used to everything, even degraded living conditions, provided that they come about slowly. The well-known example is that of the frog that leaps out when it is dropped into a pot of boiling water, but stays in it, even to the point of dying there, if the water is heated gradually. That is how Diamond explains the action of the person who cut down the last tree on Easter Island. The awareness of committing an irreparable act was clouded by habituation to earlier disasters.

The third explanation is the power that myths have over our psyche. The myth of progress that haunts Western civilization suggests that there will always be a technological solution to save humans. The rapid discovery of vaccines against Covid can only maintain that hope. We call upon the heaven of the sciences and technologies to save us from evil, the way Trump staked the epidemiological salvation of America on the promise of a rapid discovery of vaccines.

The fourth explanation given by Servigne and Stevens analyses denial as a regulative emotion, a salutary process that protects us against 'toxic information'. We know that we have to die, but we don't want to think about it every morning.

The last explanation of the denial of climate change cited by Servigne and Stevens has to do with the need to believe in an alternative solution. To react to a danger, people must be correctly informed about it, of course, but they must also and especially believe in the possibility of coping with it. This is the theory of 'groupthink' developed by Roland Bénabou. It is not enough to announce the catastrophe; to take the catastrophe seriously, we must believe that another world is possible.

Enlightened catastrophism

Jean-Pierre Dupuy wrote a book entitled *How to Think about Catastrophe: Toward a Theory of Enlightened Doomsaying*, which anticipated marvellously well the role and the dangers of collapsology in the contemporary psyche. He explains that we must really believe in the catastrophe if we want to escape it. The philosophical difficulty, obviously, is to understand how to believe in something unavoidable if the goal is to avoid it. The subtlety of the book is to lead us to grasp the import of that contradiction. It was to shed light on it that Dupuy cited Henri Bergson, for whom war appeared simultaneously 'as probable and as impossible: a complex and contradictory idea that persists until the fateful date'. In another register, but with similar intuitions, the economist Nouriel Roubini speaks of 'white swans', taking the view opposite Nassim Nicholas Taieb's famous theory of 'black swans'. For Taieb, the crisis is launched by the appearance of what he describes as a black swan – namely, an event that is a priori impossible, and that abruptly causes investors to understand that their theories are false. For Roubini, the contrary is the case: the early warning signs of financial crises are very often quite visible, but we refuse to see them.

Yves Citton and Jacopo Rasmi have written an invigorating book on collapsology, in which they stress the ambiguities of catastrophism.[10] In their view, a more accurate term for designating the current process would be 'crumbling' – like a public housing block that inevitably begins to crumble once the paint peels off and the elevator no longer works. The great risk that weighs on our material civilization is not that it will disappear from one day to the next, but that we could be led towards increasingly difficult living conditions without any possibility of turning back, except for the wealthiest, who will go to live in the north, whereas the poorest population groups living in housing projects swamped by the crisis will lose everything. 'Our societies are being split: that is probably far less striking and much more commonplace than to predict the pillage of supermarkets on the horizon of the coming decade.'

Their fundamental point is especially to show why the idea of collapse does not lead to action. People do not prevent the catastrophe, they prepare for it. It gives rise to a practice of survival: 'survivalism'. Paradoxically, the collapse comes to be *desired* by those who predict it, like the promise of messianic times. It is in this respect that collapsologists are so often annoyed by the idea that solutions exist that could ward off the predicted crisis.

This is, nonetheless, the only way open. Be scared by the looming crisis, and yet continue to hope that we can solve it.

The Society of Addiction

The effort to escape CO_2 has sometimes been compared to the battle against tobacco-smoking, as much because one finds it hard to stop smoking oneself as because of the denial organized by the lobbies. Even after research has established, beyond any possible scientific doubt, that cigarettes are a direct cause of lung cancer, they continue to be a threat. Similarly, we now know that, from the 1960s on, oil companies were well aware of the climatic risks connected with fossil fuels.

But addiction is not solely the effect of the available supply; it also responds to a demand. The use of addictive substances is committed not despite its disadvantages (including dependency), but partly because of them. To be 'addicted' to a substance or to a television series is to be relieved of serious existential problems ('Who am I?') by a process in which self-endangerment makes it possible to distract attention from the problems that sap our bases. As Christian Ben Lakhdar analyses it, the contemporary society of addiction is a mixture of several ingredients that cut across all social classes.[11] The situation of the poorest has been described by Case and Deaton's analysis of the over-consumption of opiates among the lower classes in the United States. Drugs help the poorest 'hold out' in a society that is abandoning them. At the other end of the social spectrum, there is also drug use connected with the cult of performance, to adopt Alain Ehrenberg's analysis, in which drugs become a way of over-performing, like a stock trader running on cocaine.

For economists, the use of tobacco can be interpreted as a negative sum game played between the person you are today and the one you will be tomorrow, who will pay the price of the consequences of your present addictions. It is this intellectual matrix that determines the economic analysis of the climatic risk. A harms B, he must pay the price for 'internalizing' the damage that he commits.[12] This is the 'polluter-pays' principle. If you wash your clothes at the source of a river and thereby make it unusable for your neighbours who fish downstream, you are imposing on them a damaging effect, a negative externality, for whose consequences you do not pay. Following this line of reasoning, it suffices to set a price for the cost borne by your neighbours to arrive at an efficient solution: either you stop washing your clothes, and everything is fine, or you give your neighbours the means to fish elsewhere, and the damage is repaired. In the case of global warming, the harm is imposed on future generations. Those who pollute today must be made to pay in their absence but in their name, a point that the philosopher Hans Jonas theorized in his idea of the 'principle of responsibility'.

The polluter-pays metaphor is interesting, but, in reality, it is not really suited for global warming. Price is not an end in itself, as in the polluter-pays principle, where the compensation of the polluted party by the polluting party suffices to solve the problem. The issue is not 'Pollute, provided that you reimburse those whom you harm', it is 'Don't pollute!' This is why new norms simply prohibiting cars with internal combustion engines are sometimes the most effective. However, the main issue with pricing carbon is that it assumes that the problem is already solved; it assumes that the public is in favour of it. A 'citizens' convention' held in Paris to examine this question produced a long list of recommendations, running from the prohibition of advertising to the obligation to recycle, without ever mentioning the taxation of carbon.

There are several possible interpretations of this gap between economists and the groups concerned. One is to maintain that the latter are less lucid than the experts, which is certainly what the experts themselves tend to think. Another interpretation is that the lower classes are, on the contrary, very lucid regarding the significance for them of the steps that must be taken. Taxes on fuels, like those on tobacco, are deeply regressive: it is the poorest people who pay, as a proportion of their incomes, the most. In theory, to resolve this problem, it would suffice that the public authorities promise to compensate those who suffer losses – but that is precisely the crux of the matter: people no longer believe that such promises will be kept.

Talking about the climate in general, without referring to the situation of individuals, does not work. Ecological sensitivity remains contingent upon many other parameters:

the legitimacy of public action, the intensity of the social bond, concern about future generations, etc. The place of the future in the imagination of each individual is not the same from one segment of society to another. When your vocation or your social environment (e.g., the fact of living far from large cities) dooms you to social death, it is hard to rise above your present condition in the name of the well-being of future generations.

The climate is not a new religion, and not even a substitute for the latter in the secular world we live in. It does not escape the usual categories of political life. When we examine voters' preferences, we observe in this domain a scattering of opinions that is very close to their general political position. Regarding the battle against global warming, left-wing voters are most favourable to it, right-wing voters are much less favourable, and the far-right voters are the least concerned. Those who were counting on unanimous support in favour of climate action had to lower their sights. For most people, ecology was important, but no more than the healthcare system or purchasing power.[13]

Awareness of the climate catastrophe has certainly increased. Surveys show that three-quarters of the French now think global warming is a serious threat and that it is the result of human actions. But between those who are ready to count on technological progress to find solutions, and those who want to begin living in a survivalist mode immediately, the range of opinions is so broad that it is difficult to feel reassured regarding humans' collective ability to agree on the steps to be taken. The perverse role of the digital revolution – sorting people into a multiplicity of groups – makes it even harder to share a common roadmap.

The problem is greatly complicated by the fact that it is not solely a matter of reconciling the self that we are today with the one that we will be tomorrow. This reconciliation must take place here and now at the level of the whole planet.

Poor countries that aspire to catch up with wealthy ones find it very hard to accept that they should forgo a car and meat because of damages for which the wealthy countries are themselves to blame. The French can be convinced by sobriety (banish planes and meat), but if the Chinese, the Americans, or the Indians do not agree, it will be of little use. We would like to think that the climate offers humans access to a sort of universal awareness of their common terrestrial dimension. We are still very far from that.

The solution, however, for every individual and every nation, is to explore alternatives to the current model, and show that they can be desirable. We must feel not only sadness on contemplating a world that is splitting, but also joy in the one that is possible. A smoker who gives up tobacco has to think that he is regaining the means to lead a healthy life, otherwise he is merely living in mourning for a lost happiness, and a relapse is inevitable.

7

In a Hundred Years

The Society of Abundance

According to anthropologist Marshall Sahlins, hunter-gatherer societies enjoyed abundance and insouciance, working only 2 to 4 hours a day to feed everyone.[1] This is the world that existed prior to the Malthusian curse – that of a truly abundant society. Anthropologists have re-examined the general validity of Sahlins' picture. The idea that hunter-gatherer societies did not work hard and did not accumulate wealth is not universal. The gatherers of northwestern California, for example, were known for their cupidity. According to Graeber and Wengrow, 'their life was organized around the accumulation of money (in the form of shell money) and sacred treasures, and the rigorous work ethic they had developed was directed toward this single goal'. Humans did not wait for agriculture to appear before exploring all the possibilities of social life.

Yet agrarian societies did change the mentality of humans. The Malthusian curse made life much more difficult. Working harder and harder to feed a growing population became the norm. Things started to change only in the late nineteenth century. With the rise of industrial society, a major shift occurred that turned humans away from the agrarian mentality. After 10 millennia, during which these societies fabricated a system of subjecting women to the demographic imperative, the birth rate finally collapsed, first in Europe, then in the rest of the world. A project conducted by demographers at Princeton University yielded a multitude of results in this domain. In a few decades, from 1870 to 1910, a decrease in fertility occurred in almost all European countries, concomitantly and almost independently of socio-economic variables. For example, England and Hungary began their transition at the same time, even though they were very different in terms of education and infant mortality. Bulgaria, which was illiterate and rural, began its transition at the same time. This simultaneity leaves hardly any doubt regarding the fact that this is a cultural phenomenon much deeper than a simple reaction to socio-economic evolution connected, for example, with urbanization.[2]

The same turning point was observed in developing countries. The fall in fertility was manifest in a few decades, passing from 5 children per woman on average in 1950 to 2.4 today. The explanation given by the demographers of the United Nations agrees with the conclusions of the Princeton Project on the European transition. Its sources are cultural. Women all over the world saw on television a model that fascinated them: that of Western women whose (televisual) way of life became for them an aspiration to freedom. The Brazilian *telenovelas* proved stronger than the Church, which had nonetheless succeeded in blocking family planning.[3] The demographic transition is explained by a change in mentality, not a change in financial incentives. To project ourselves into a desirable future, we must imagine a change of the same kind, a new transition from quantity to quality.

The great hope of the twenty-first century

Writing in 1928, the eminent British economist John
Maynard Keynes announced a great hope for the twenty-
first century that echoes, in an astonishing way, Marshall
Sahlins' description of 'wild societies'. 'In a hundred years',
he wrote – and we are almost there – 'three hours of work
per day will suffice to satisfy the old Adam in us.'[4]

A century has passed and we are still grappling with the
economic problem. Today, consumption is four times higher
than it was in the 1960s, and yet we do not feel happier.
How is that possible? An initial response is that capitalism
knows how to whet people's appetite for consumption,
offering goods whose possession quickly becomes indispensable even if they were unknown a short time before.
This inventiveness of capitalism is its strength. To it we owe
the cinema, the telephone, the washing machine – all items
whose original intended use contributed to human progress.
The problem is that beyond the need itself, we always have
to go further – to have the latest model of car, iPhone, etc.,
to avoid losing status. This is the famous theory of 'keeping
up with the Joneses', which transforms society into a field
of permanent rivalries. The economist Richard Easterlin is
associated with this paradox of a kind of wealth that never
succeeds in making people happy, so sapped are they by
their constant comparison with others.

However, something more powerful has begun to operate
since the publication of Keynes' book, which fulfilled his
prediction almost tacitly. If we confine ourselves to the goods
that characterize consumption at the time when Keynes wrote
his essay, the end of work has in fact taken place! The shares
of industry and agriculture now represent no more than 15
per cent of the hours worked in a country such as France
or the United States, as compared with 60 per cent when
Keynes published his essay. The disappearance of industrial

society has occurred! As Jérôme Fourquet has pointed out, vestiges of it remain in a society in which the shopping centre has replaced the factory as the popular imagination's construction site. But everything that used to constitute the heart of mass consumption – household appliances and television – now represents no more than a marginal share of expenditures. We no longer buy industrial goods because we desire to have them, but far more in order to get new ones when the old ones no longer work. The irrepressible decrease in their price makes it simpler to buy a new television set when the old one breaks down, which helps us to understand here the usefulness of carbon pricing to avoid this waste.

The composition of private expenditure allows us to follow the extraordinary transformation of modes of consumption that has taken place over a half-century. Items like food and tobacco, combined with basic industrial products, clothing, and home appliances, represented more than half of expenditures in 1960. Today, they account for less than a quarter.[5] In contrast, the two budget items that exploded were housing and cars, whose combined share doubled in the course of the same period. Today, these two items represent 40 per cent of total consumption.[6] The Yellow Vests made the indivisible unity of these two budget items clear. In response to the increasing costs of housing, the lower classes sought to maintain the size of their living space by moving farther and farther from their workplace. Hervé Le Bras has stressed this astonishing fact: despite the immense disparities of income between the wealthy and the middle and lower classes, one budget item resists these inequalities – the number of square metres occupied by the two groups. The richest do not occupy much more space than the poor: everything plays out in the location of residence. One group lives in the fashionable neighbour-hoods, in the centre of the city, and the other has to travel much farther to reach its workplace.

These questions have little relationship to those for which traditional industrial growth provided answers. It is not by increasing the production of television sets or washing machines that the difficulties of the popular classes will be solved. In fact, we have to fight the obsolescence of goods, be sure that they are made from recyclable materials, and consume less. The great question of post-industrial well-being lies elsewhere. It depends on where you live, with whom your kids interact, and that is something that growth does not change.

The role of public spending is another major characteristic of post-industrial society, at least in Europe. In France, its share almost doubled in the course of the last sixty years, rising from 5.5 per cent to 14 per cent of the total expenditure. The fact that healthcare or education is provided, in France, mainly by the public sector and paid for by taxes creates a confusion that leads people to say everything and anything. A classic argument is that a dynamic private sector is necessary to pay for public spending. Do we have to sell toothpaste in order to pay physicians? That is obviously idiotic. We can (mentally) imagine a society where everyone would be a physician or a nurse, where the purchasing power created by working was saved, so that people could take care of themselves when they were old or sick. This system could just as easily be public (in France) as private (in the US). What counts is not the origin of the production, but the well-being that it provides for people.

However, whether the care economy is private or public does affect the way the 'cost disease' is dealt with. One terrible example has shown the dangers inherent to cost-cutting when it comes to humans. Orpea is a French company whose mistreatment of elderly people shocked the whole of France and bluntly raised the fundamental question: what does productivity mean when it is a matter of caring for human beings? We can imagine reducing administrative costs, the way Watson, the assistant created by IBM, can make it unnecessary to hire assistants. But in the end, when it's a question of taking care of people themselves, every gain in productivity threatens to dehumanize an activity whose heart is the care provided by one person for another. In the case of Orpea, the inquiry's report sends shivers down your spine. It was reported that meals lacked meat; that snacks were not systematically provided during the evening, so that periods without eating that were longer than the recommended 12 hours were frequently observed. Everything was done to reduce the number of staff. According to the lawyer for the victims, residents were put to bed at 4 p.m., to reduce the time spent with them. Wheelchairs were used to simplify moving the patients, with the foreseeable effect that they quickly lost their motor abilities.

The relation to humans cannot be managed in the same way that the materials of industrial society were managed. If digital society is the way to make service activities productive, then lines must be drawn that cannot be crossed when it is a matter of caring for people. In fact, productivity itself becomes a very bad indicator of what is meant to be achieved.

Back to Science Fiction

The film *Elysium* holds up a mirror to the society whose advent we would absolutely like to avoid. The elites have migrated towards a planet orbiting the Earth, where peace and prosperity reign. Robots and autonomous military drones deal with the plebs, who have remained on Earth. *Elysium* pushes to its extreme this vision of a society in which the rich enjoy a numerous staff of servants for all their needs, whereas the masses, at the other end of the chain, is handled by robots and algorithms.

Science fiction (SF) likes to represent a world crushed by over-population, socially polarized by exiling of the rich or of the poor to other planets. The economy plays a central, underlying role in this. In SF stories, 'corporations' are often more important than states or governments (when the latter are even represented!). In *Ubik*, a book by Philip K. Dick, the author of *Blade Runner*, the currency is called 'poscreds' and serves to pay for everything: the front door that opens automatically to give us access to our homes, the refrigerator that feeds us, etc. – all ways of reminding us that everything has a price, that every act is measured by the yardstick of its commercial value. In Andrew Niccol's film *Time Out*, the currency is time itself. People don't work for money, but for seconds, hours, years of life. In the film's opening scene, a son rushes towards his mother to give her the minutes she lacks, but in vain. The rich person is one who has a life that is counted in centuries.

SF returns us to the beginning of modern political economy in the seventeenth century, when the first thinkers such as Quesnay, Smith, Malthus, and Ricardo were looking into the source of wealth: is it land or labour? SF replies in a very modern way: it is raw materials and technologies that count, while human labour, which is supposed to be superabundant (via the myth of over-population), falls very far down the scale of constraints. Is SF's imagination only a reflection of our fears, or does it foretell a possible world, a world that could even be inspired by it? In his time, Jules Verne perfectly anticipated a number of inventions that were to be introduced later on. His work is, moreover, cited by the economist Robert Gordon as witnessing to the idea that the consumer society that asserted itself all through the twentieth century was foreseeable from the early 1900s. The fundamental great turning points, electricity and the internal combustion engine, were completely visible at the dawn of the past century, just as are microprocessors and AI today.

To anticipate the development they announce, it suffices to apply to the whole of society the ruptures that are already there in germ.

Closing our eyes, we can thus imagine a world where face recognition will replace showing one's passport in airports or standing in line at the supermarket; where algorithmic management will put an end to traffic jams, thanks to autonomous vehicles communicating with each other; where apps will permit self-medication except in serious cases, when the physician will be immediately alerted; a world where banks without automatic tellers will monitor your accounts in real time, and whose algorithms will offer you credit at rates reflecting a financial score that is constantly updated. This vision might seem all the more irrepressible because technologies now tend to be produced without consulting their main users. Ford conceived assembly-line work for factories of which he was the project manager. Today, apps such as Booking.com or Uber have revolutionized sectors of which they had, a priori, no knowledge whatever. As Tristan Harris, the president of the Center for Humane Technology, wrote, 50 designers make decisions for 2 billion people.

Wisdom and beauty

However, it is possible to convince yourself that SF's imagination is not the right one. What is rare and precious is not robots or raw materials; it is humans, the quality of their social life. In 1968, Robert Kennedy gave a famous speech that still resounds just as strongly today:

> The gross national product does not allow for the health of our children, the quality of their education or the joy of their play. It does not include the beauty of our poetry or the strength of our marriages, the intelligence of our public debate or the integrity of our public officials. It measures

neither our wit nor our courage, neither our wisdom nor our learning.

A study of unequalled depth admirably confirms Robert Kennedy's intuitions. In an international comparison of the determinants of satisfaction with life in different societies, Richard Layard and his co-authors have shown that the most subjective factors – trust in others, generosity, and health – are elements of well-being that are much more decisive than the GDP itself.[7] On a scale of 1 to 10, doubling an individual's income increases his well-being by 0.21 points. A sunny day does better than that! Living in a couple rather than alone increases the level of well-being by 0.8 points. Interpersonal trust and generosity are more crucial factors: on the same scale, trust is capable of increasing well-being by a full point, five times more than income. Moreover, a lab experiment showed that people were made happier by giving them 100 euros to donate to good causes than by an offer to let them spend these 100 euros on themselves.

In any case, the direct effect of income on well-being is not a sufficient measure of its real impact. It must be corrected to take into account the 'negative externality' represented by the enrichment of others. When wealth does not consist solely in buying objects but in holding a place in society, or even just being able to rent the work-time of a person who takes care of you, the contribution of an increase of income to well-being is reduced by the enrichment of others. Rare things such as a well-placed residence in the city centre remain just as difficult to obtain if the income of other inhabitants is also increasing. To a large extent, wealth is a relative matter: getting rich is a good thing, but it's especially good if others are deprived of it! Here, France is again an astonishing country. While the French pride themselves on adhering to a 'logic of honour', statistical analysis shows that in reality they are very sensitive to material wealth – far more, for example, than the English or the Germans.[8] One possible explanation for this is that the French find it very hard to live together. Money is the last remedy of a society struggling to unite its members.

An essential point of Layard's book bears on problems of mental health. The latter is the main cause of inequalities in well-being. The study sets forth an analysis of incredible profundity by following *all* the children born in Bristol between April 1991 and December 1992. It allows us to study their development, in an almost exhaustive way, in relation to all the possible parameters: their parents' situation, the schools they attend, including the teachers themselves. Unsurprisingly, the children's trajectory depends to a large extent on their parents' social milieu. On the other hand, the fact that a mother works does not influence her children's grades. What counts far more is the emotional state of the mothers. It directly influences that of the children, even if, surprisingly, the mothers' mental health seems not to play any role in determining the children's grades at school. A fascinating result of this study is to show that the teacher plays a role that is almost as important. Good teachers have a much more fundamental impact on the child's emotional development than they do on their grades! An attentive teacher will, obviously, improve a pupil's grades in mathematics or literature, but the mark he leaves on these domains is transitory. What remains, sometimes throughout a pupil's life, is the influence a good teacher can have on children's psyche. Depending on whether he gives them self-confidence or not, whether he provides them with the emotional resources for a calm relation with others, they will become accomplished or unhappy adults.

I cannot resist citing here once again the letter that Albert Camus sent to his high school teacher after he won the Nobel Prize: 'When I heard the news, my first thought, after my mother, was about you. Without you, without the affectionate hand you offered to the poor child that I was, without your teaching, and your example, none of all that would have happened.'

Maternal love

It is with teachers like Camus's, caregivers devoted to their patients, and honourable politicians that we can organize the resistance to what we must call the issue of the century: the systematic digitalization of human relations. Numerous studies show the inanity of projects that seek to substitute algorithmic intelligence for human sensitivity. Michel Desmurget, whose study of the 'digital cretin' we have followed, has also analysed MOOCs (open online courses). An investigation carried out on a million users shows that they have 'relatively few active users, that the users' engagement diminishes considerably, especially after the first two weeks of a course'. Nor have MOOCs succeeded in attracting poor and under-educated students, even though it was thought that the latter would be their chief beneficiaries: about 80 per cent of the people who signed up for courses online already had a university diploma.

Desmurget also emphasizes another fundamental limit that the digital tide does not seem capable of transcending, even if he adds 'for the moment': maternal love. Babies discern very clearly the difference between the human relation, typically that of the love that their mothers give them with their bodies, and what a video of the same thing can offer them: 'For reasons that remain to be explained, the stimulations are far from having the same impact, depending on whether they are addressed to infants by humans or by machines.' Desmurget cites an experiment conducted by Pier Francesco Ferrari, an expert on social development among primates who sought to analyse experimentally the way in which empathy functions.[9] To save time, Ferrari decided to replace the experimenter with a video of him. In a completely unforeseen way, the result was catastrophic: it was as if the mirror neurons, which are the foundation of empathy, had been unplugged when a flesh-and-blood person was replaced by a film.

Another experiment reinforces this conclusion. Professors tried to teach Mandarin to 9-month-old American babies. As in Ferrari's (unintended) experiment, some of the babies were taught by a human being, and the others by a video of the same professor, teaching exactly the same things. The result: education by video turned out to be totally sterile. The imperceptible but decisive bond that leads the teacher to pause when the child winks his eyes, to modulate his voice in response to the emotion that he discerns in his pupil, was lacking between the video and the child. The video does not respond to the emotional messages that the baby sends, and this lack of sensitivity is probably reciprocal: understanding that the video does not respond to his own emotions, the baby loses interest in it.

This example is emblematic of the risks that digital society makes us run. It cuts the tie that permits a human being, when he is faced by another human, to think that this other human knows, or thinks he knows, what he himself is feeling. Desmurget concluded his splendid study on a disabused note. Perhaps, he writes

anthropomorphic robots will one day be able to raise our children in our place, interpret their babbling, feed their curiosity, watch over their slumbers, smile at their mimicry, hug them ... A child without all the bother, descendants without the burden of bringing them up. Google and its algorithms will take care of everything: the best of all possible digital worlds!

By Way of Conclusion

The digital society promises the end of hierarchies, and in certain regards it delivers. On the social network, everyone can say whatever he wants. Within firms, a new horizontality has emerged. We can be equals, call each other by our first names, but only within a strictly homogeneous professional circle. A new type of society arises that is based neither on individualism nor on the hierarchical model of earlier societies. A kind of 'collective individualism' emerges when we espouse the identity of a group to which we want to belong.

Addiction and surveillance are the two key dangers in this new world. In one of the episodes of *Black Mirror*, which is among the most painful ones to watch, a computer's camera observes a young man who has been filmed while watching videos for child abusers that he has obtained online. As the guardian of morality, the algorithm leads him to murder another offender by threatening to reveal his hidden life. This sequence illustrates the perversity of digital society. It puts under supervision an individual that it makes addicted to its own products. These 'psychic contradictions' prolong the 'cultural contradictions' of industrial capitalism – namely, an incitement to debauchery in the order of consumption, and an iron discipline in the order of production. In digital capitalism, this tension is pushed to the point of absurdity: to compulsive addiction on the one hand, and to the surveillance of individuals' slightest actions on the other.

The digital economy is replacing the old industrial order that prevailed with the Fordist revolution. The latter ended up exploding in the course of the 1960s, when youth in revolt challenged the discipline imposed in factories and universities as much as it did the gloomy and repetitive character of consumer society itself. The problem that the 1960s had not been able to resolve was that of finding an alternative society to establish. Hippies and leftists explored new ways of living in 'communities', from Larzac in France to the suburbs of San Francisco. Alas, as the sociologist Bernard Lacroix brilliantly showed, what was magnificent in the summer turned into a nightmare in the winter, as it did in hunter-gatherer societies whose way of life changed radically with the change in seasons.[1] 'The sun, you see, with really nice people: living in a cool way, far from the city, without having to go to work every day', wrote one of them in his diary, on 26 July 1972. On 19 January of that same year, he had written in a different vein: 'It's very cold … I don't agree anymore! I'm not made for a monk's life! … I don't want to be penned up with animals … There are plenty of things to see elsewhere, and I don't want to cut myself off from them.' Lacroix explains perfectly why most of these communities did not survive the erosion of time. In archaic societies, the individual has virtually no option to leave; his beliefs incorporate the constraints of the world in which he has to live. In a monastic community, getting in is the hard part: you have to prove that you're worthy of belonging to it. Once accepted, the newcomer wants to live up to the efforts made and the expectations raised. In the communities created in the 1960s and 1970s, people went in and came out as they wished: no glue held its members together over time. When winter came, they lost heart and everything had to be rebuilt.

It is in the hollow of these failures that the digital revolution bloomed. Its pioneers were often former protesters dreaming of creating a world without hierarchy, without the principle of obedience. At the origin of the Internet, there was the Arpanet network, created by the American Department of Defense, the legend being that it was supposed to make it possible to protect the communications system from an enemy attack. However, this system was extended to universities, which turned it into a key instrument for their interactions. University campuses are the living laboratory of new technologies. The academic world is itself the implicit model of the society that is trying to find its place in the digital revolution. Like the bonobos, scientists are, above all, a cooperative species. They share the results of their research, and are always prompt to write articles with co-authors from other universities, other countries. Like ancient Greeks in the city-states, they confer the administrative responsibilities on their different members alternately, sometimes through a lottery.

But academics are also in competition – sometimes ferocious or petty – to publish the article that will be cited first on this or that subject. The academic community revealed itself to be vulnerable, much more than it is prepared to admit, to the competitive pressure that the digital revolution itself has generated. Online rankings of researchers in relation to the number of times their works are cited have become common currency. One click on Google Scholar makes it possible to find out where an academic stands relative to his colleagues. That whets an intense rivalry that did not exist before. A study of the University of California, Berkeley, showed the shock represented by the online publication of each faculty member's salary, the professors ranked lowest feeling humiliated by the shameless display of their 'market value'.

However, what welds together this strange community is a dimension that seems very naïve when seen from outside: something like a common faith in science. A scientist can allow himself to say whatever he wants, provided that his theory is falsifiable by experimentation or opposable by the contrary arguments of his peers. That is the 'meta-narrative' of a possible science that binds together the members of this community. Academic life offers an almost perfect ideal type of the 'good society' that is sought by the digital revolution: simultaneously horizontal and secular. In it, hierarchies are weak, at least relative to what they are in the rest of society: during a seminar, a young researcher can at any time question his master. And it is secular in the refusal constitutive of its identity: the rejection of any revealed truth. Its problem is that the price of entry is very high, in the way in which one used to belong to a medieval monastery. How many theses, studious readings, and meticulous experimentations fill the cemeteries of university lives? And the academic model is profoundly endogamous, recognizing as legitimate only the judgement of peers. In that regard, it is perfectly in phase with the culture of associating only with people of the same ilk that the digital world has established, perhaps in its image.

Despite their weaknesses, universities have nonetheless provided the realized model of a society in which each individual is listened to and respected, and which is imbued with a common confidence in the values on which it is founded. The challenge that the contemporary world must answer is to extend this idea to larger social groups of society.

In the domain of political life, we must have no illusions regarding the ability of social networks to produce by themselves an alternative to the traditional parties. The latter had the merit of reconciling different social universes, the worker and the teacher on the left, the bourgeois and the peasant on the right, and of seeking a balance between dream and reality across broad social groups. In the digital era, politicians are able to aggregate only a much smaller fraction of the electorate, united by hate speech against others. On election night, only 25 per cent of the voters are really happy with the results. The others feel they have been deprived of their rights. Social networks will never solve the problem. What is necessary is to reconstruct inclusive institutions fighting social disparities. The days when the Church or the Communist Party could aggregate the faith of large fractions of society will never return. We need to be more modest. But universities, hospitals, post-industrial unions, and a post-'fake news' press can help to reinvent institutions that people can trust. The idea that we can do without them, that individuals only need to communicate with one another, is the illusion that the digital revolution entertains – the trap that has to be avoided.

Notes

Introduction

1 Genesis 27:22: 'The voice is Jacob's voice, but the hands are the hands of Esau.'

1 Body and Mind

1 Thanks to Professor Benabid's team in Grenoble. The direct brain–computer interface can be more or less invasive, using electrodes implanted directly in contact with the brain, or simply a helmet fitted with sensors.

2 *Le Monde*, 4 December 2020. (Unless otherwise stated, translations from foreign-language publications are by Steven Rendall.)

3 F. Wolff, *Le Monde à la première personne. Entretiens avec André Comte-Sponville*, Paris : Fayard, 2021.

4 A. Prochiantz, *Singe toi-même*, Paris: Odile Jacob, 2019.

5 R. Dunbar, *How Many Friends Does One Person Need?* London: Faber and Faber, 2011.

6 Game theorists have analysed the implications of this in models said to be at K-levels (level-K theory).

7 N. Huston, *The Tale-Tellers: A Short Study of Humankind.* Toronto: McArthur & Co., 2008, pp. 27–8.

 8 M. Benasayag, *The Tyranny of Algorithms*, trans. S. Rendall, New York: Europa, 2019, p. 14.

 9 The book *The Affect Effect*, ed. W. R. Neuman et al. (University of Chicago Press, 2007) lists twenty-three theories to explain the possible connection between affect and cognition!

10 Symmetrically, hatred is a sadness that is accompanied by the idea of an external cause. Satisfaction is a joy that is accompanied by the idea of an internal cause. Remorse is a sadness that is accompanied by the idea of an internal cause.

11 The primary emotions arise in the first year of life, while the moral emotions appear only between 18 and 24 months. Starting at 21 months, babies have a sense of the just and the unjust.

12 Since the works of the anthropologist Ruth Benedict on Japan, we distinguish the pair culpability/pride from the pair shame/honour. The first term designates the moral value that we assign (directly) to our own acts, the second has to do with the idea that we form concerning the judgement of others. See R. Benedict, *The Chrysanthemum and the Sword* (1946; rpt Boston, MA: Mariner Books, 2006).

13 D. Kahneman, O. Sibony, and C. Sunstein, *Noise: A Flaw in Human Judgement* (Glasgow: William Collins, 2021).

14 Daniel Kahneman et al., *Thinking: Fast and Slow* (2012).

15 D. Kahneman and A. Tversky, 'Judgment under uncertainty: heuristics and biases', *Science*, 1974.

16 M. Mézard, in *Le Débat*, 207, 2019-5, sums up the question in an illuminating example. An algorithm may be capable of simulating perfectly the trajectory of a ball, on the condition that it has been made to digest millions of kicks of the same kind. But it will nonetheless be incapable of correcting the predicted trajectory if the ball is hit by another one. Scientific knowledge doesn't have this problem: it transposes knowledge to unprecedented situations – it is adjustable.

17 Max Tegmark gives this analogy: over the past fifty years, the cost of information has dropped to such an extent that the city of New York would cost its owner only 10 cents if the same reduction were applied to it – it would be 10,000 billion times

less expensive than it is in reality. The cost of calculation is reduced by a factor of two every eighteen months. 'Or a million millions (10^{18}) since my grandmother was born', he adds.

18 Contrary to legend, Einstein's brain weighed only 1.23 kilograms, compared with an average of 1.4–1.5 kilograms.

19 The whole chain of living beings, from the earthworm (exactly 302 neurons) to the orangutan (32 billion neurons), functions on this same model.

20 *Marianne*, 15 April 2022.

21 Of course, AI can paint or compose music, but it does not know whether the result is beautiful: only a human can decide that question.

2 Stultify and Punish

1 B. Patino, *La Civilisation du poisson rouge*, Paris: Grasset, 2019.

2 G. Bronner, *Apocalypse cognitive*, Paris: Presses universitaires de France, 2021.

3 Ibid.

4 Ibid. Frances Haugen also notes that Facebook did in fact modify its algorithms ahead of the 2020 presidential campaign, in order to reduce the quantity of 'fake news' that they allowed to be posted. As soon as the election was over, however, the company is supposed to have immediately reconfigured them as they had been before. According to Haugen, that might be what facilitated the assault on the Capitol on 6 January 2021. And we do not know if we should laugh or weep, but a message in English stating that 'all vaccines for Covid are experimental, the people vaccinated being part of the experiment', has been viewed more than 3 million times, whereas it was supposed to be taken down. The cause of this malfunction: the automatic tool thought the message was written in Romanian.

5 H. Allcott et al., 'The welfare effects of social media', *American Economic Review*, 110(3), March 2020.

6 J. Soler, quoted by Bronner, *Apocalypse cognitive*.

7 B. Jarry-Lacombe et al., *Pour un numérique au service du bien commun*, Paris: Odile Jacob, 2022.

8 E. Illouz, *La Fin de l'amour*, Paris: Le Seuil, 2020.
9 N. Chuc, *Le Figaro*, posted online 9 January 2022.
10 A. Mitchell and L. Diamond, 'China's surveillance state should scare everyone', *The Atlantic*, 2 February 2018.
11 Google, Apple, Facebook, Amazon.

3 Waiting for Robots

1 L. Devillers, *Les Robots émotionnels*, Paris: Éditions de l'Observatoire, 2019.
2 M. Ford, *Rise of the Robots: Technology and the Threat of a Jobless Future*, New York: Basic Books, 2015.
3 This is called 'the Cambrian explosion'. See G. Pratt, 'Is a Cambrian explosion coming for robotics?' *Journal of Economic Perspectives*, August 2015.
4 At the Georgia Tech Center, cited by Ford, *Rise of the Robots*.
5 Kahneman et al., *Noise: A Flaw in Human Judgement*.
6 É. Sadin, *L'Intelligence artificielle ou l'enjeu du siècle*, Paris: L'Échappée, 2018.
7 A. Supiot, 'Restaurer un travail réellement humain est sur le long terme la clé du succès économique', *L'Usine nouvelle*, 24 April 2015.

4 Political Anomie

1 Over the past fifty years, the wage of a white male without a university education has lost 13 per cent of its purchasing power (after correcting for inflation).
2 It is only in the second half of the nineteenth century that real wages started to rise significantly. Between 1840 and 1880, the productivity of labour increased by 90 per cent, and real salaries by 120 per cent, according to the figures given by R. Allen in *Engels' Pause: A Pessimist's Guide to the British Industrial Revolution*, Oxford University Press, 2007.
3 P. Askenazy, *La Croissance moderne: organisations innovantes du travail*, Economica, 2002.
4 M. Pak, P. A. Pionnier, and C. Schwellnus provide an excellent

survey of these questions in *Économie et statistique*, nos. 510–12, an issue on the fiftieth anniversary of the journal, which itself offers a magnificent synthesis of the developments during the last five decades.

5 G. Cette et al., in *Économie et statistique*, nos. 510–12. The share of revenue going to the top 1% has, however, risen from 7% of the total to 10%. The purchasing power of the richest 1% increased from 2.2% per annum, compared with less than 1% for the remaining 99%. See, in the same issue, B. Garbini and J. Goupille-Lebret.

6 The productivity of labour, which epitomizes the progress of technologies, has moved from a rate of growth of 4.5% per year from 1960 to 1975, to 2.1% from 1974 to 1992, then to 1.1% from 1993 to 2008, before almost dying in 2008 at a rate of +0.6% per annum from 2008 to the present.

7 Polarization of labour markets has been documented in the US by D. Autor and D. Dorn, 'The growth of low-skill service jobs and the polarization of the US labor market', *American Economic Review*, 103 (5), 2013, 1553–97; in the UK, by M. Goos and A. Manning, 'Lousy and lovely jobs: the rising polarization of work in Britain', *The Review of Economics and Statistics*, 89 (1), 2007, 118–33; and in France, by A. Resheff and F. Toubal, *La Polarisation de l'emploi en France*, Paris: Cepremap, Éditions Rue d'Ulm, 2019.

8 D. Acemoglu, 'Good jobs and bad jobs', *Journal of Labour Economics*, 2001.

9 S. Beaud and M. Pialoux, *Retour sur la condition ouvrière*, Paris: Fayard, 1999. As Goux and Maurin also show, a large number of young people who have a university education have had to resolve to take jobs that do not require their level of training, thus competing de facto with less educated young people, who have thus experienced an unforeseen contest that drives their remuneration lower: *Économie et statistique*, 510–12.

10 C. Baudelot and R. Establet, *Suicide, l'envers de notre monde*, Paris: Fayard, 2006.

11 L. Rouban, *La France: une république désintégrée*, Paris: Sciences Po–CEVIPOF, 2021.

12 J. Fourquet, *L'Archipel français*, Paris: Le Seuil, 2019.

13 J. Fourquet and J.-L. Cassely, *La France sous nos yeux. Économie, paysages, nouveaux modes de vie.* Paris: Le Seuil, 2021.

14 M. Gentzkow, 'Polarization in 2016', Stanford University, 2020.

15 G. Ward et al., '(Un)happiness and voting in the US presidential election', *Journal of Personality and Social Psychology*, 2021.

16 R. Inglehart and P. Norris, *Cultural Backlash: Trump, Brexit and Authoritarian Populism*, Cambridge University Press, 2019.

17 This is notably the thesis presented in 'Identity, beliefs and political conflict', by G. Bonomi, G. Tabellini, and P. Gennaioli, *Quarterly Journal of Economics*, 2021.

18 Y. Algan et al., *Les Origines du populisme*, Paris: Le Seuil, 2019.

19 Y. Algan et al., 'The European trust crisis and the rise of populism', *Brookings Papers on Economic Activity*, 2017.

20 D. Reynié (ed.), *Où va la démocratie? Une enquête internationale de la Fondation pour l'innovation politique*, Paris: Plon, 2017. All the following figures are taken from this collective work.

21 C. Mudd, 'The paradox of the anti-party party: insights from the extreme right', *Politics*, 2 (2), 1996.

22 B. Jarry-Lacombe et al., *Pour un numérique au service du bien commun*, Paris: Odile Jacob, 2022.

23 H. Allcott et al., *American Economic Review*, 2020. The experiment asked, in return for remuneration, a group of 2,743 people to disconnect from Facebook for four weeks before the American mid-term elections in 2018.

24 M. Gentzkow, 'Polarization in 2016'.

25 E. Vul and H. Pashler, 'Measuring the crowd within', *Psychological Science*, 2008.

26 See M. Ottaviani and P. N. Sorensen, 'Information aggregation in debate: who should speak first?' *Journal of Public Economics*, 2001.

27 J. Cagé, *Essays in the Political Economy of Information and Taxation*, Paris: EHESS, 2013.
28 R. Bénabou and J. Tirole, 'Mindful economics: the production, consumption and value of beliefs', *Journal of Economic Perspective*, 2016; R. Bénabou, 'Groupthink: collective delusions in organizations and markets', *Review of Economic Studies*, 2013.
29 Obviously, the question of the reality principle arises. Am I putting myself in danger by believing this or that absurdity?
30 According to a study cited by Bénabou, more than 80 per cent of the population is affected by this optimistic bias.
31 Loewenstein and Molnar show that you really want others to think the way you do, and the moral fact that in your view they are in error annoys you. According to the law named after Cunningham, one of the founders of Wikipedia, one of the best ways to get a good answer is to propose a bad one: that immediately triggers a desire to answer it.
32 A. Molnar and G. Loewenstein, 'Thoughts and players: an introduction to old and new economic perspectives on beliefs'. In J. Musolino, J. Sommer, and P. Hemmer (eds.), *The Cognitive Science of Belief*. Cambridge University Press, 2022, pp. 321–50.

5 Social Ties

1 To be precise, the maniple oscillated, depending on the period, between 120 and 200 soldiers.
2 The estimates vary from 4.7 to 3.5, depending on the study.
3 E. MacLean, 'Unraveling the evolution of uniquely human cognition', *PNAS*, 113 (23), 2016.
4 N. Jacquemet, *Comment lutter contre la fraude fiscale?* Paris: Cepremap, Éditions Rue d'Ulm, 2020.
5 The book by S. Asma and R. Gabriel, *The Emotional Mind: The Affective Roots of Culture and Cognition*, Cambridge, MA: Harvard University Press, 2019, analyses many of the debates that we take up here.
6 One of the unchanging traits of happiness is the ability to trust

others. The French are less happy on average, in large measure because they suffer from a rather systematic lack of confidence in others.

7 In *Plaidoyer pour l'universel* (Paris: Le Seuil, 2011), Francis Wolff shows that reciprocity is the foundation of ethics: minds endowed simply with dialogic reason would agree on rules of reciprocity.

8 See J. Elster, *Le Désintéressement*, Paris: Le Seuil, 2011.

9 Quoted in Asma and Gabriel, *The Emotional Mind*.

10 'Bullshit' has become a philosophical term since Harry Frankfurt, a professor at Princeton, published *On Bullshit*, Princeton University Press, 2005.

11 P. Seabright, *The Company of Strangers*, Princeton University Press, 2004.

12 *The Situation Is Hopeless but Not Serious: The Pursuit of Unhappiness*, New York: Norton, 1983.

13 I. Kadaré recounts the appalling history of this phenomenon in his book *Broken April*, Sami Books, 2001.

14 H. Simon, 'Organizations and markets', *Journal of Economic Perspective*, 1991.

15 Bénabou, 'Groupthink'.

16 Economists call this disposition – wanting to recoup the fruits of an investment, even in situations in which that has become irrational – the 'sunk cost fallacy'. If, for example, you go to see a play and it bores you, you'll nonetheless stay until the end if you've paid a high price to see it. If, on the contrary, someone else has paid for your ticket, you'll leave at the intermission. One or the other of these attitudes is not 'rational'.

17 Thus, one study has shown that divorces were more frequent at the top of the economic cycle: women who work are more prompt to ask for a divorce when the job market is tight.

18 D. Graeber and D. Wengrow, *The Dawn of Everything: A New History of Humanity*, London: Allen Lane, 2021.

19 J. Cauvin, *Naissance des divinités, naissance de l'agriculture*, Paris: Editions du CNRS, 1994.

20 As Michael Kremer shows, the rate of population growth itself grows with the size of the population, a recipe for an explosive

process: M. Kremer, 'Population growth and technological change', *Quarterly Journal of Economics*, 1993.

21 The idea of a rigid division of labour in which males were hunters and females gatherers has been contested by anthropological research that has found many proofs that female hunters existed. See Vivek Venkataraman, 'Women were successful big-game hunters', *The Conversation*, 10 March 2021.

22 Yves Lambert, *La Naissance des religions. De la préhistoire aux religions universalistes*, Paris: Armand Colin, 2007.

23 In his book *Naissance des divinités*, he shows, by dating made possible by carbon 14, that the appearance of new religious practices preceded agriculture. Alain Testart is more prudent in *Avant l'histoire*, Paris: Gallimard, 2012.

24 J. Bottéro, *Lorsque les dieux faisaient l'homme*, Paris: Gallimard, 1989.

25 Judaism itself went through two stages. Initially, it was based on two pillars: the Temple and the Torah. For a long time, being a Jew meant making offerings to God, and having animal sacrifices made by the priests, like most of the ancient religions. With the second destruction of the Temple by the Romans, the rabbis gained power over the priests. Henceforth, being a Jew meant studying the Torah and its commentaries. The link with ancient religions was definitively broken. Botticini and Eckstein's account shows that the obligation to read (which was very expensive in the agrarian society of the time) was going to provoke an abrupt decline in the number of Jews. Their book, *The Chosen Few* (Princeton University Press, 2012), recounts this attrition, which was to be interrupted only with the development of cities such as Baghdad and Cordova, where Jews were to learn how to valorize their religious ideal in this new urban world.

26 C. Taylor, *A Secular Age*, Cambridge, MA: Harvard University Press, 2007; 2018.

27 M. Jensen and W. Mekling, 'Theory of the firm: managerial behavior, agency costs and ownership structure', *Journal of Financial Economics*, 1976.

28 N. Bloom et al., 'Firming up inequality', *Quarterly Journal of Economics*, 2019.

29 P.-A. Chiappori, 'Theory and empirics of the marriage market', *Annual Review of Economics*, 2020.

30 It is obviously conceivable that it is the countries where tolerance is great also make the integration of groups possible. However, there are econometric methods for getting around this obstacle. By exploiting the fact that the minorities who live close to borders resemble those who live on the other side of the borders (in an exogenous way), the authors verify that the causality goes in the right direction. Cf. A. Banerjee and R. Pande, 'Parochial politics: ethnic preferences and political corruption', CEPR Discussion Paper, 2007, quoted by A. Alesina and K. Zhuravskaya, 'Segregation and the quality of government in a cross-section of countries', *American Economic Review*, 101 (5), 2011.

31 F. Jameson, *Postmodernism, or, The Cultural Logic of Late Capitalism*. New York: Verso, 1992.

32 Perrine Simon-Nahum interprets it as a new nihilism: *Les Déraisons modernes*, Paris: Éditions de l'Observatoire, 2021.

33 California was the first to force Uber to include drivers among its salaried employees.

34 The idea of a social rating of companies has already been mooted, but it remains embryonic, and, above all, it has no legal impact on the life of enterprises.

6 Winter Is Coming

1 A study done by the Conseil d'analyse économique shows that countries' resilience when facing the crisis was closely linked to the quality of individuals' confidence in their public institutions or in their own fellow citizens. See Y. Algan and D. Cohen, 'Les Français au temps de la Covid: économie et société face au risque sanitaire', *Les notes du conseil d'analyse économique*, 66, 2021.

2 Y. Algan et al., 'Trust in scientists in times of pandemic', *Proceedings of the National Academy of Science*, 2021.

3 It is difficult to get people to admit that there is a difference between a programme of scientific research that always remains

open-ended, on the one hand, and the established facts of scientific theories (gravitation, microbes), on the other.

4 M. Dewatripont, 'Vaccination strategies in the midst of an epidemic', Brussels: CEPR, 2021.

5 In all, since 1850, Europe and North America have emitted 39 per cent of the total, Asia 20 per cent, and Africa 7 per cent.

6 The emissions of greenhouse gases are 54% higher than they were in 1990. Their rate of growth has slowed, to be sure, passing from 2% in 2000–9 to 1.3% in 2010–19, whereas the energy intensity of the growth (CO_2/GDP) is decreasing by 2% a year. The IPPC is calling for an effort seeking a 50% reduction in emissions between now and 2030. The peak of pollution has to be reached by 2025 at the latest, and emissions have to decline afterwards, reaching zero in 2050 at the latest to remain below the target of 1.5 °C. To limit warming to 2 °C, this target would have to be reached in 2070.

7 Their cost has already decreased a great deal. The cost of solar energy has fallen by 85%, wind energy by 55%, and lithium batteries by 85%. Obviously, we lack efficient methods for storing energy, and research into hydrogen and innovative batteries must also be increased.

8 In 2019, 34% of net emissions were produced by the energy sector, 24% by industry, 23% by agriculture (in the broad sense), 15% by transportation, and 6% by construction. If we impute energy to its users, 34% of net emissions came from industry and 16% from construction, the energy sector itself falling to 12%.

9 P. Servigne and Raphaël Stevens, *How Everything Can Collapse: A Manual for Our Times*, trans. A. Brown, Cambridge: Polity, 2020.

10 Y. Citton and J. Rasmi, *Générations collapsonautes*, Paris: Le Seuil, 2020. Dupuy himself further discussed the abusive uses of catastrophism in *La Catastrophe ou la vie*, Paris: Le Seuil, 2021.

11 C. Ben Lakhdar, *Addicts. Les drogues et nous*, Paris: Le Seuil, 2020.

12 The pricing of carbon would also make it possible to avoid

a fatal trap: the increase in the power of renewable energies might cause the price of fossil fuels to fall, thereby contradicting the initial objective.

13 As the Covid crisis was easing, the French ranked purchasing power at the top of the list of concerns, with 44% of the respondents, healthcare with 33%, and the climate with 32%, even though 77% of French people say they are convinced of the climate risk.

7 In a Hundred Years

1 M. Sahlins, *Stone Age Economics*, New York: Aldine-Atherton, 1972.

2 A. Johnson Coale and S. Cotts Watkins, *The Decline of Fertility in Europe*, Princeton University Press, 1986. France, which was a pioneer in this domain, began its demographic transition at least a century before other European countries, even before the Industrial Revolution and mass urbanization began. Conversely, the demographic decline of England began years after the emergence of large industrial cities.

3 See Eliana La Ferrera et al., 'Soap operas and fertility', *American Economic Journal: Applied Economics*, 4 (4), 2012.

4 J. M. Keynes, 'Economic possibilities for our grandchildren' (1930), in *Essays in Persuasion*, rpt New York: Norton, 1963.

5 Food and tobacco fell from 32% to 19.5%, clothing from 12% to 3%, and home appliances fell tom 8.5% to 4.5%.

6 Cars rose from 10.5% to 14% of expenditures, while housing rose from 11.5% to 26.5% (heat and light included).

7 R. Layard et al., *The Origins of Happiness*, Princeton University Press, 2018.

8 D. Cohen et al., *Les Français et l'argent*, Paris: Albin Michel, 2021.

9 Empathy is triggered by 'mirror neurons', thanks to which a subject (human or simian) swallows when he sees one of its congeners drinking a glass of water, or is hungry when he sees eating. We integrate the behaviour of others into our psyche,

as if the action of others, and the situation in which they find themselves, were in part ours as well.

By Way of Conclusion

1 B. Lacroix, *L'Utopie communautaire: Mai 68, l'histoire sociale d'une révolte*, Paris: Presses universitaires de France, 1981.

Index